FINDING A

NEW NORMAL

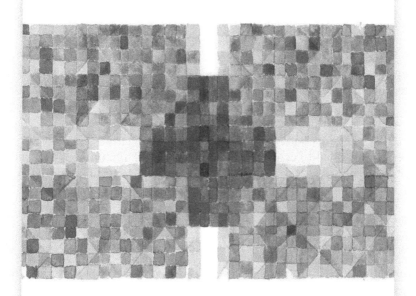

PERMISSION TO BE REAL IN YOUR GRIEF

RAY LEIGHT

FINDING A
NEW NORMAL

PERMISSION TO BE REAL IN YOUR GRIEF

RAY LEIGHT

TABLE OF CONTENTS

DEDICATION

I would like to dedicate this book to all the people who have experienced traumatic loss. I hope that in some way this resource helps bring freedom and peace to you.

ACKNOWLEDGEMENTS

We are truly grateful to all who helped us in our time of loss. It was a very emotional and enriching experience to be showered with love and support during our grief. I would love to list you all here, but there were so many who stepped up anonymously and gave generously to help, it wouldn't be possible. Thank you, we love you and appreciate you.

I now have a greater understanding and respect for all the first responders who give so much to serve the community. The hard work and sacrifice they give is humbling. The traumatic loss they encounter daily is almost unimaginable. If you are a first responder, I pray that you and your families will be richly blessed with peace, love, grace, and hope.

NOTES FROM THE AUTHOR

Thank you for trusting me to help you walk through your grief. This book is inspired by what I have learned over the years from processing through my own trauma and loss, as well as helping thousands of people work through some of the most traumatic and painful experiences of their lives. I hope this book will bless you and give you permission to be real in your grief. Blessings and peace to you as you walk through your losses, trauma, or grief.

Blessed are those who mourn, for they shall be comforted.

Matthew 5:4

CHAPTER ONE

THE AFTERMATH

When piecing together the fragments of your life after experiencing a tragic loss, it can seem almost like you are walking around in one of those apocalyptic movie scenes, confused and unsure of where you are or what happened. It's OK, there isn't something wrong with you. All of us have experienced loss in some way. Something traumatic happened and you are now in the process of establishing a new normal. You may still be in the beginning of this process, or you may have had some time to sort out your thoughts and emotions. Most likely, if you are reading this, you have already experienced the initial shock of loss and are beginning to move forward. Regardless of where you are in your personal process, it is a very challenging and emotional experience. Take your time and allow yourself to grieve. Grief is not something you need to be healed of—grieving is the process of healing.

When we are in the aftermath of a traumatic loss, the initial response is commonly a time of shock. In this early stage of the grieving process, we will also experience a sense of denial. Shock and denial are usually working together. What happened is more than we can handle, and we go numb. We don't just disconnect from the loss, sometimes it seems that there is a disconnection from reality itself. It is so hard for us to accept that what happened really did happen. Denial is almost an automatic response to the situation. Again, there is not something wrong with you if you have experienced this or are now experiencing it. Loss is traumatic. When we are traumatized by loss, we experience a sense of shock and denial. The intensity of this experience can be surprising and unexpected. You may need help to get through this.

My hope for this book is to help you be honest with yourself, and with God, as you intentionally process the different aspects of grieving. It is too much to process all at once, and you will eventually be able to face the different emotions you have from your loss. The shock will pass, and the denial can end. That does not mean you will ever understand what happened or be OK with it. The reality is, you will never be the same again. Your life will never be the same again. This does not mean you won't be OK.

As you go through your grieving journey, it can seem very confusing and lonely. As much as it may feel like you are alone, please know that you are not. There are so many who have suffered loss, understand grief, and are available to help. You have permission to feel and experience grief in your own way. It will be a unique journey for you, not exactly the same as anyone else's grief. In the following chapters we will walk through some of the different aspects of the grieving process. I will also share some of my story and some practical tips that may help you.

I'll start with the loss that inspired this book ...

My wife, Kathryn, and I were on our way back home to Redding, California, from a vacation with friends. We landed at the Sacramento Airport very late on a Wednesday night. Because we were flying all day and getting in so late, we planned on staying the night at a hotel and then driving the two and a half hours home the next morning. We got to the hotel around 1:00 a.m. and finally got to sleep around 2:00 a.m. We woke up early the next day to head home. This was when we found out that the city we call home was on fire and that our neighborhood had been evacuated.

I'd heard about a fire in Northern California, miles away from our neighborhood on the other side of Whiskeytown Lake. At that point, I didn't even know it was a serious fire. I had no idea this seemingly far off threat had grown out of control during the night and was racing toward Redding, with our home in its path.

We got ready to leave as quickly as we could and headed back to Redding. To say we were in a daze when we got back in town is an understatement. The smoke was the worst I had ever seen. Ash was falling like rain, and the sky resembled a real-life experience of an apocalyptic movie. The fires were still spreading and the tension and uncertainty in the city were as thick as the smoke. It seemed like the end of the world had arrived in Redding. We spent the night with our daughter, who had a place on the east side of town, away from the fires.

The fires were out of control and ravaging everything in their path. They had even jumped the Sacramento River and were heading for the city. Neighborhoods and homes were being consumed by fire, and people were being evacuated all over town. We spent the day trying to figure out what to do next.

That afternoon someone told our son about videos updating people on the status of their homes. He found the one updating the status of our neighborhood, and we all sat down to watch it together. At this point we were still hopeful that our home had survived the fire.

I still remember all of us sitting at my daughter's house, watching the footage. We watched as the man in the video drove up the road of our neighborhood. We were nervous and holding on to hope as we saw the destruction that used to be our neighbors' homes. It was tense and exciting as he drove up our driveway. Then the video panned left toward where our home was located. That is when it hit. There was no house there. I felt the impact in my whole body. I went numb and didn't know how to respond. Our two cars were visible in the driveway, burned to bare metal, partially melted and almost unrecognizable. Behind them was a pile of rubble barely viewable in the distance. I could see the smoky sky where the house used to be. It took a few minutes of shock before I connected with the magnitude of the loss. The reality of it hit me, and I broke. I was overwhelmed and began to cry uncontrollably. This was the beginning of my grieving journey.

The fires were still largely uncontained, and the atmosphere of fear and uncertainty in the city was too much for us to handle. We couldn't stay in Redding anymore, so we relocated to Sacramento. We spent two weeks in Sacramento before we returned, uncertain of what we would find. Our neighborhood had been quarantined and inaccessible the whole time we were away. Amazingly, the day we came back was when they opened our neighborhood. We drove right to where our home used to be. I thought this was going to be a painful and overwhelming experience. Surprisingly, it was refreshing to go there and be able to see in person what we had only seen in a rough video. Oddly, it helped in the process of grieving to be able to tangibly see the destruction.

Redding was still a challenging place to be during this time. The air was still toxic, and the emotional impact was depressing. Everything seemed difficult. Even finding a place to temporarily live was problematic. We stayed in Redding long enough to go through the ash-out process, which involved digging through the rubble and remains of the house to see if we could find anything that survived to fire. The ash-out was difficult for me because there was nothing left that had emotional value. It was very disheartening that everything was destroyed. The fire was extremely hot at our home and it disintegrated almost everything. I was in a real place of discouragement, feeling unloved by God and angry that this had happened.

While going through this, I had asked the Lord to let us find something that would make me feel loved. I had completely given up on this and was just trying to accept the total and absolute loss when, out of the blue, I got reminded of God's love. I was driving with my son when he opened up the glove box of his car, pulled out a burnt piece of paper, and showed me what he found. He and our daughter had gone to the location one last time before we left town. They were walking on a trail just above where the house used to be when they noticed a piece of paper. It was a single page from one of my books. Somehow the Chapter Eight title page, "Repent and Believe," from my book *Identity Restoration* survived the fire.

This was a miraculous and almost unbelievable answer to my prayer. This restored hope in me and helped me to experience and feel the love of God. He made it personal, and in the remains of a 3,000 degree fire that destroyed our entire home, He allowed us to find this glimmer of tangible hope. Don't get me wrong, this didn't fix everything. Even though I felt loved in that moment, I still had a lot to process.

PENT AND BELIE

have intentionally stayed present, chosen
cted with God. We have acknowledged the presenc
r thoughts and our feelings, right in the situation w
taken inventory of our hearts. We found out the trut
ny lies we believe, and the self-protections we are u
out what we would have if we didn't believe the lies an
to self-protect. We have also forgiven anybody connecte
at needed to be released. Now it is time to repent from
ceive the truth.

e time is fulfilled, and the kingdom of God is at
ent and believe in the gospel. – Mark 1:15

ty to apply the kingdom principle of repentance will
your life.

he definition of "repent" and then exami
nition.

filled, and the kingdom of God is at h
ts, repent, think differently, and belie

s calling us to change our thinking. T
is about thinking, not behavior. This is
ommended that we choose reality in the
ctually think our thoughts. You cannot reco
aving, repent from it, and think differen
re what you are thinking. This is why repen
ectical and sustainable lifestyle of freedom an

You cannot reconsider a thought you are having
repent from it, and think differently, if you
won't acknowledge what you are thinking."

1:15, the Lord is telling us to reconsider the lies we b
erently, and believe the good news. Changing our thin
fferent than changing our behavior. Focusing on and
our behavior, instead of focusing on the thoughts
g that behavior, is not repentance and will not help
freedom.

y arguments and every lofty opinion raised
re of God, and take every though
ians 10:5

CHAPTER TWO

THE FOG

The fog. If you've ever experienced the dizziness and confusion that can happen after a traumatic loss or event, you've known the fog.

It is a weird experience similar to the initial shock and disconnection from the trauma, though it is not quite the same. It can be described many ways. It is like a confusion, dizziness, and inability to think properly all at the same time. Some directly relate this to depression, though I see it differently. I have personally walked around like a zombie, unable to think properly or make decisions after a loss. I have also worked with clients who were experiencing this same aspect of grieving.

I believe one of the reasons for the fog is a result of our inability to comprehend loss. We were not created to ever experience loss. I don't think we will ever understand it, or that it will ever make sense to us. Loss is not an aspect of the kingdom of God. It is an unnatural part of life that is a result of the fall. God's original design for us was to live and live abundantly. As the Word tells us in 1 Corinthians 15:26, death is an enemy that will be destroyed. In God's perfect design, there is no death, there is no loss. We were created for life and abundance, not loss.

The level at which we experience this fog seems to be directly connected to the level of how much our lives are affected by the loss. What I mean by this is we all have a desire for stability, consistency, normalcy, and familiarity. It seems that when our hearts and minds are thrown into a turmoil after a traumatic loss, they are on overload trying to process and reestablish those levels, those normals. The more the trauma has disrupted these normals, the more overwhelming the reestablishing process is for us.

There are multiple forms of loss that we experience throughout our lives. Some will affect us greatly, and some will just be a minor adjustment. And no, it doesn't always make sense why we are affected as little or as much as we are.

During the grief process, we are internally trying to comprehend something that will never make rational sense. The loss we experienced does not fit in our understanding and we are using all of our internal resources to get back to a sense of normal. This overload causes an inability to have the mental capacity available to manage complex thought processes and make decisions. The difference for me between this and depression is the absence of thought. It is not an inability to think properly because of an overflow of unhealthy thoughts, which can be a sign of depression. It's that there are no thoughts, no room for thinking. This overwhelming experience of trying to reset to a new normal seems to be an automatic process. It runs in the background of our minds, using up our natural thinking and reasoning abilities.

It is almost as though our minds and our hearts are continually processing, consuming the resources we would normally use to make decisions and choices in our lives. All the energy and memory needed to have complex thought is being exhausted through this process.

Different types and intensities of loss will affect us differently. I have experienced many forms of loss, though the loss of my home impacted me more than all the others I had previously experienced. How much the loss affects you doesn't have to make rational and logical sense. Just let yourself process what is actually happening. Even though the grieving process you are experiencing is not unusual, the way that it is affecting you personally is unique to you. The events of your life, your beliefs, and your willingness to face the pain all influence your unique experience.

It is OK that you don't understand any of the "whys" of the loss you have experienced. Allowing yourself to not have to understand it will help you move forward and begin the process of reestablishing connection to your new normal. Trying to understand the loss can get you stuck in a loop of pain and confusion that can lead to depression. It is not about forgetting or denying. It is about accepting your new reality and allowing yourself to be OK, even in this new unfamiliar place where nothing is OK.

There is not something wrong with you or your faith. Experiencing this fog, caused by the trauma of your loss, is not an indication of you being unspiritual. Wherever you are in whatever grieving process you may be in, just know you are not alone. Everyone experiences grief from loss. Not everyone is willing to face their pain and process their loss. Your willingness to face it is courageous and will help you get through it.

I personally walked around in this fog for about a month after the house fire. One of the ways this affected me is that it was difficult for me to go into stores. Any time I had to process a lot of options and make a decision, my brain would stop working properly. I would become over-sensitized and would have to get out of the store. It was similar to a panic attack, though I do not remember feeling any fear. It just seemed like there was too much information coming at me all at once, and I could not process it. One of the most intense experiences of this was in Costco. There was a moment when all the colors in front of me, which made up the perspective of the store and the people I could see, started separating and no longer looked like reality. It was like a Disney Fantasia scene where all the colors in front of me became distorted and started to mix together and move around. It felt like I was going to pass out. It all happened so fast I didn't even have time to freak out. Thankfully, I began to recognize my daughter and then was able to refocus and be OK. That was the only time it was that extreme. All the other times, I have been able to realize what was happening early on, and just leave the store.

Throughout this process, even after the cloud seemed to lift, I have had times of re-experiencing the fog. When I need to make multiple, complex, or analytical decisions, my brain will begin to shut down. These moments of being over-sensitized are happening less and less, but it still affects me sometimes when having to make decisions with many options.

You may be, or you may have been, experiencing some type of fog yourself. There is no need to panic. You will be OK. If possible, hold off on decisions that do not need to be made immediately. I recommend finding people you can trust to help you work through some of the choices that need to be made. As much as you can, let others help you when you have trouble being decisive. If you do not have people around you who understand you and whom you can trust, a therapist or grief group may be beneficial for you.

You may even experience a sense of frustration and impatience with yourself as you go through the fog. This may be causing your life to be at a slower pace than you are used to. It's OK, let yourself rest and recover as you need. There is no need to rush your process and force yourself to do things that are too much for you right now. As much as possible, intentionally try to be patient with yourself and your present condition.

Give yourself grace and patience while you are processing through the fog. I believe it is very important to allow yourself time to recover. You can do this, and you will be glad you did.

CHAPTER THREE

WHEEL OF EMOTIONS

Most likely you are familiar with the commonly accepted stages of grief. They are: shock, denial, anger, bargaining, depression, testing, and acceptance. The term "stages" can be misleading because it can imply that grieving is a seven-stage sequential process. I would recommend thinking about them as "aspects" of grief. Grieving isn't a seven-step process. The different aspects of grief can happen in almost any random order. Also, within each aspect, there are many different emotional responses that can happen. I describe this as the *wheel of emotions*.

As we are experiencing life after a loss, it can feel out of control and overwhelming. We won't know what will trigger an emotional experience. At any moment, something can initiate the spinning of the *wheel of emotions*, which leaves us waiting to see what it lands on. This process can be particularly frustrating when we are still in the fog and are not operating at our full capacity. The random triggering and spinning of the wheel can feel like an emotional roller coaster ride. You just have to hold on the best you can.

I have found, both in my own experience and in working with many others, that if we are willing to stay present mentally and emotionally, and process what the wheel lands on, we can experience freedom. If we face it and allow ourselves to work through the emotion, we won't have to re-experience the same level of painful impact from the same issue over and over again. This takes an intentionality that we don't always have the energy or mindset for, because of the loss.

We will experience the holistic enormity of the loss, as well as the individual, smaller aspects of the loss. What I mean by this is, with a major traumatic loss, we are not processing just one simple loss. Every relationship we have has various dynamics to it. Each one of these dynamics can initiate the spinning of the wheel and give us the opportunity to face the emotional response it lands on. The more intimate our relationship, the more dynamics involved.

For example, the death of someone we love will cause multiple layers of grief. There is the direct loss of that person, and the loss of the different aspects of the relationship. Some of the possible aspects of the loss could include:

- Future plans you had with them
- Hopes and dreams you had with them
- Needs they fulfilled for you
- Rituals and habits you had with them
- Memories and experiences you had with them
- Familiar things that remind you of them
- Relationships you shared with them

These are just a few of the possible connections with someone that can cause pain. At any moment, a reminder of any one of these connections can trigger us into the loss again and initiate the spinning of the *wheel of emotions*. We don't choose these moments. It can be rather annoying as we are going about our day and randomly get triggered. The instability of the roller-coaster ride of emotions can even cause us to question our sanity. It is OK if this is happening to you! You are not crazy; you're grieving. It is a lot of work to intentionally stay present in your thoughts and emotions and process the aspect of the loss that gets triggered. Believe me though, it is worth it.

Wheel of Emotions

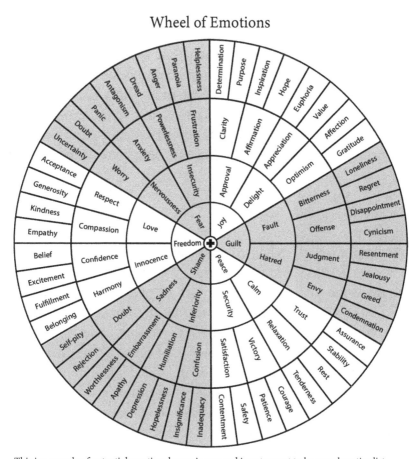

This is a sample of potential emotional experiences and is not meant to be an exhaustive list.

I remember being frustrated that I was still going through this process. I think we were about two or three weeks out from the house fire when I no longer wanted anything to do with the grieving process. I wasn't anywhere near done with grieving, but I was done with having to be in it. The emotional roller-coaster ride that it seems like we are stuck on is not convenient to everyday life. I understand why people attempt to distract themselves from the emotions or try to deny what is happening.

As we experience the overwhelming nature of the loss, we will also be reminded of the different relational dynamics of our loss. These multiple reminders will impact us in varying degrees. At any point, these reminders can trigger us into any one of the emotions. We are familiar with the common emotions of sadness, anger, fear, and loneliness, but we are not limited to these. As you can see from the emotional wheel, there are many to choose from. Each one of these can fit into the various aspects of grief. We land all over the place on this spinning *wheel of emotions* throughout the process. It seems to be much worse in the beginning of our grief, leaving us feeling quite unstable.

For me, experiencing this wheel was almost like a random, unexpected punch in the gut. The simplest things would trigger me. For example, one time when Kathryn and I were out shopping for kitchen supplies, she asked me if I wanted a new meat tenderizer. Boom, there it was! That simple question triggered me into the grief and loss all over again. The meat tenderizer we lost in the fire was my grandmother's. It was this old, one-piece, heavy chunk of metal that I was fond of. I immediately flashed to the memories of my grandmother and was sad, then angry, then sad, then frustrated. No, I didn't want some cheap meat tenderizer. I didn't even really want a meat tenderizer at all. I only had one because it was my grandmother's. This was just another reminder of a cherished memorial stone that used to bring fond memories and emotions. Now it was gone. I didn't even remember the meat tenderizer until Kathryn asked me if I wanted a new one. This was one of those times when I wasn't ready to take an emotional roller-coaster ride. I just wanted to get some supplies and get out of the store.

The goal is not to be unaffected by the memories of our loss. I don't think we ever completely get over it. This meaningful part of our life is now gone. That will never change. I do think it is possible for the painful impact to become less impactful as we allow our hearts to process the pain and loss. Instead of holding on to the painful emotions as a connection to who we lost, or what we lost, we can begin to reconnect to the fulfilling emotions of why we cared in the first place. This may even feel dishonoring at first. Sometimes it can seem like we are being uncaring, or unloving, if we are not feeling bad from our loss. This is not true. Your love for someone or something is not determined by how bad you feel when you experience loss. Yes, you will feel bad and you probably do, but you do not need to feel bad forever. We don't have to lose our future because of loss in our past. You may not be in a place yet where you can accept that. This is OK. Don't deny where you are in your grief.

As much as you can, let yourself experience the emotions you are experiencing, and invite the presence of God to meet you in those emotions. His presence will comfort you. If you are having trouble with this, don't worry. I have found that we even protect against God's presence sometimes because of our hurts, wounds, and beliefs. Don't think there is something wrong with you if you have trouble connecting with God in your grief. You are not the only one. It is more common than you would think. When you are ready, you can begin to work through the thoughts you have in those emotions. If you need help understanding how to intentionally stay present in your thoughts and emotions, and how to process through your grief, my book *Identity Restoration* is a helpful resource that will walk you through this.

CHAPTER FOUR

LONELINESS

Loss can be an extremely lonely place. It doesn't matter who you're with, where you are, or how much you are being cared for. The feeling of loneliness can completely overtake you during the grieving process and affect you in ways that do not appear to fit the situation.

I remember shortly after we lost our home in the fire, when we were staying in a hotel, I began to feel isolated and lonely. It didn't make sense at all. Hundreds of people had reached out to us. I was regularly receiving phone calls, texts, and messages on social media. Our needs were covered, we were together as a family, and we were all safe. Right in the middle of all this, I felt completely alone.

It is important to realize that even if you experienced your loss with others, you can find yourself feeling completely alone. It can feel like no one else understands or knows what you are going through. As much as people may try to connect and relate to you, it can prove difficult. This is a sad and scary place to be.

It is not uncommon for people in the grieving process to experience this. If you have been feeling like this, it's OK. You are not alone, and you are not the only one who has felt this way. I think it is helpful for you to know that it's OK. This loneliness isn't rational, and it doesn't have to last forever. These shifts and changes are one of the aspects of grieving. As we looked at in Chapter Three, the emotions and experiences continue to change throughout the process.

It is true that no one else has ever had your exact set of life experiences and losses. There are so many relational dynamics and variations in each of our lives. There is no one person who can perfectly relate to us and our loss. That is why it is so crucial to allow God to meet us in that place of loneliness. He is the only one who fully knows and understands our loss.

> He was despised and rejected by men, a man of sorrows and acquainted with grief; and as one from whom men hide their faces He was despised, and we esteemed Him not. Surely He has borne our griefs and carried our sorrows; yet we esteemed Him stricken, smitten by God, and afflicted. But He was pierced for our transgressions; He was crushed for our iniquities; upon Him was the chastisement that brought us peace, and with His wounds we are healed. – Isaiah 53:3-5 ESV

The Word says the Lord is acquainted with and has borne our griefs. He is the one who can carry our sorrows and bring us peace. Let's look at the definitions of "acquainted" and "borne" and then examine the Scripture in light of these definitions.

Acquainted – the Hebrew word used here is **yada`** (Strong's H3045)

It means: to know – to be known – experiential knowledge – to make known – comprehend – be aware of – be acquainted with

Borne – the Hebrew word used here is **nasa`** (Strong's H5375)

It means: to lift – bear – burn – accept – carry – forgive – help – raise – receive

An expression of the Scripture including the fullness of these definitions could be:

> *He was despised and rejected by men, a man of sorrows, and is acquainted with, aware of, has experiential knowledge of, and comprehends our grief; and as one from whom men hide their faces He was despised, and we esteemed Him not. Surely He has received, accepted, forgiven, lifted, and borne our griefs and carried our sorrows; yet we esteemed Him stricken, smitten by God, and afflicted.*

The Lord is acquainted with, knows, has experiential knowledge of, and comprehends our grief. He has received, accepted, lifted, and carried away our grief and sorrow. He knows your grief, understands your situation, and can help you with your sorrow.

The Lord is the only one who can truly relate to us and help us in our loneliness. If we allow ourselves to be present in the loneliness of loss and connect with the Lord in our thoughts and emotions, we can begin to move toward the peace and healing that is available in Him.

I don't think anybody enjoys feeling lonely. It is understandable that you may want to distract yourself from the loneliness you are experiencing or deny it in some way. Unfortunately, this will not help. Denying your feelings, distracting from the loneliness, and pretending like everything is OK can inadvertently establish a foundational lie that you are alone. This lie can cause you to isolate yourself and secretly live a life of sadness and loneliness, regardless of what is happening and who you are with. This foundational loneliness can slowly steal the remaining relationships and abundance of life you have after the loss you've just experienced.

The enemy is lying to you and trying to steal, kill, and destroy your joy, peace, and freedom. One of the tactics to accomplish this is to help you establish those foundational lies and keep you sad and alone. You will most likely feel sad and alone after a loss, this is common in the grieving process. Who or what you lost is gone. This is a devastating reality. This is not something you can change. You won't have what you lost, but you can have your freedom, peace, and joy again.

As miserable as it is to experience the loneliness and sorrow, it is important to let yourself be present in it and let your heart work out the loss. This will help you connect with the true value of your loss, process the actual loss, and learn how to live in your new reality. Yes, this sucks! There is nothing fun about facing the emotional anguish of no longer having what you once had. Remember, it will never make sense. You may never understand why this happened, or why it can't just be the same as it was. Allowing yourself to face what happened, and what is happening with you now, will help you return to a sense of peace in your new normal. If you find yourself stuck in a loop of isolation, depression, or loneliness, I recommend pursuing help outside of yourself. It is OK to need help. It can and does get better.

CHAPTER FIVE

WHEN GRIEF FEELS HOPELESS

The loss of a loved one, an important relationship, a dream, or something you deeply cherish can be devastating. It can take you to a place of hopelessness and depression you may think will never lift. This is not an uncommon experience in the grieving process. It is inevitable that there will be times of depression after a significant loss. The intensity and frequency of the depression and hopelessness will vary.

The sadness can be extreme as you realize your life will never be the same again. All the memories, experiences, and emotions connected to your loss can flood through your mind and contribute to the experience of hopelessness. The weight of all this can seem unbearable. You can begin to lose purpose. It can be difficult to find inspiration for your career, dreams, relationships, or day-to-day life.

You may find it difficult to get yourself motivated to do things like leaving the house, going shopping, or even getting out of bed. Regular tasks that you didn't even notice in the past, can become difficult and emotionally overwhelming. Days can blend together as you seem to just be surviving from moment to moment. Everything can seem to be meaningless and irrelevant.

This is a very sensitive issue that not everyone is willing to admit. Especially in some social circles, depression can be regarded as a weakness, or lack of faith. As we discussed in Chapter Four, your friends and family may not understand or know how to help you through this aspect of grief. It may even be a challenge for you. You may have never experienced the level of sadness and hopelessness you are now experiencing. There is not something wrong with you if you are experiencing this.

I have found that if you are willing to intentionally stay present in the depression, think your thoughts, feel your emotions, and process your hopelessness with God, you can naturally move forward and not stay stuck. You may not have the energy or motivation to do this at first. It is very helpful to be honest with yourself and others you trust and allow yourself to be comforted. If you don't have safe people around you who can comfort and care for you, it may be helpful to find a grief group or a counselor. Allow yourself to just take the steps you can to move forward.

Times of depression are an aspect of the grieving process. It is important to remember that the grieving process shifts, moves, and changes. It is not a consistent feeling. One of the ways to see if you are simply grieving, or if you are stuck in depression, are the emotional shifts. The depression in the grieving process does not last forever.

Being honest with yourself about how you are feeling will

help you process through the grief. The unhealthy cultural expectations around us can sometimes cause us to try and deny the depression, put on a performance for others, and try to make it appear like everything is OK. Denial is not rooted in faith. The unfortunate and misguided teachings that encourage a denial of your emotions, and the idea that you just need to have faith, are not encouraging faith. Denial is rooted in hopelessness. It is a result of not believing there can be true resolution. Encouraging this type of thinking is not healthy or helpful. Denying the hopelessness and depression, and not allowing yourself to process your emotions and thoughts, can establish foundational lies that will linger. Even Jesus experienced emotional sadness around death and loss.

> When Jesus saw her weeping, and the Jews who had come with her also weeping, He was deeply moved in His spirit and greatly troubled. And He said, "Where have you laid him?" They said to Him, "Lord, come and see." Jesus wept. – John 11:33-35

If we look at this Scripture in the context of the whole gospel message, we will see it more clearly. Jesus, the King of Kings, was already seated in heavenly realms with Lazarus and was getting ready to raise him from the dead when He was deeply moved, greatly troubled, and wept. If it is OK for Jesus to respond to loss in this way, I believe it is equally OK for us to respond this way.

I lived much of my life denying my emotions and stuffing them as much as I could. Instead of dealing with my pain, I tried various methods of numbing it. It never worked, even though I tried to convince myself it did. I would even say things like, "Deal with it," or "Get over it," when someone was actually processing their issues. I have found that people who talk like this are neither dealing with their issues nor getting over them.

I had an experience that I share in the first chapter of my *Identity Restoration* book. This experience ripped the lid off the emotions I had been stuffing for years, and they all came pouring out. It was overwhelming and I ended up going into a complete depression. It was miserable.

Allowing myself to be present in this depression and process with God changed the entire course of my life. I experienced freedom, peace, and joy in ways I never knew were possible. Freedom is available. It is possible to experience peace and joy again. It is OK that you may not be experiencing it right now. You do not need to pretend or rush the process. Back when I was stuck in hopelessness, I would get angry when people would talk about how they got free from something. I had such foundational hopelessness that I couldn't celebrate other people's victories. I would get jealous, bitter, envious, and angry that other people could be free, and I couldn't. It was not a fun place to be.

It didn't all happen at once for me. It has been many encounters, trials, challenges, and learning experiences that have contributed to the freedom I now live in. Part of that freedom is an ability to not have to perform for others. If I am in a bad place, I do not pretend I am happy just to make others more comfortable. I am also not accepting the negative emotions as a normal way of life. I live a life pursuing freedom, peace, and joy while intentionally acknowledging and processing any guilt, fear, or shame that is happening.

Although hopelessness and depression are common after a loss, they are not your new normal. They are part of the grieving process that will help get you to your new normal. There will even be random times when you trigger into them, even after you think you are doing OK. Freedom, peace, and joy are possible again. Settling into the deception that you will always be depressed is very dangerous. Even though you may think that you can't go on, or you can't live without someone or something, the truth is, you can. You have what it takes to get through this. The Lord is acquainted with your grief and He can comfort you in this. You may be in a place where you don't see the hope right now, but don't give up. Hold on, hope is possible again.

My life is the evidence that there is hope. I had such a core, foundational hopelessness and loneliness established in my heart. I never thought it would change. I didn't know what it was like to be anything other than alone. I had friends and relationships, but I was always alone inside. There are moments when I can remember how bad it was, but for the most part I can't even connect with it anymore.

One thing I do to help remind myself of hope, is to remember the memorial stones of change in my life. For you, the grief may be too recent, and the pain may be too much for you to celebrate the good things of who, or what, you just lost. If you can, try to look back at previous victories in your life before your recent loss. Focus on where you have been able to reconnect with the goodness of what you lost and celebrate what you had. This is an exercise I use with my coaching clients to help them when they are stuck in sadness and hopelessness. I have found this to be a very effective tool in renewing thought processes. Ask the Lord to remind you of these victories and allow yourself to be encouraged in the Lord. This will strengthen you, and help you establish your new normal.

CHAPTER SIX

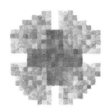

SHOULDA, COULDA, WOULDA

In this chapter, we are going to explore the aspect of the grieving process commonly referred to as the bargaining stage. This is one of the more dynamic aspects of the process. We can go from fantasy negotiations, to replaying all the possible scenarios, to looking at all the things that should have or could have been done differently—all the while attempting to escape from the reality of what happened. I see this as a more imaginative way to use denial. I think this connects with our inability to understand or accept the loss we just experienced. It is interesting to me how we can go from the original shock and denial into a type of intellectual denial through the fog, and then into this more imaginative denial. This aspect of denial can cause the exhaustive emotional roller-coaster ride that we looked at in Chapter Three.

"If only" is one of the common thoughts in this aspect of the process. If only I had ..., if only they had ..., if only I knew ..., if only ..., if only ..., if only! It can go on forever. It seems there is a never-ending list of possible scenarios and options about how it could have been different. We don't want what happened to be true, so much that we fantasize about how it could be different.

You may or may not experience this aspect of the grieving process. This might not be your coping mechanism, but many of us will experience this in some way after a loss. The frequency and intensity at which each person experiences this will vary.

You may find yourself exploring all the different options in the fantasy of outcomes, or you may focus on one specific thing. I think the response you have in this area depends on your emotional and relational upbringing. For me personally, I tend to get angry with myself and God when things go wrong. I don't waste my time on other people, I go right to the top. When I experience loss, I don't dwell on what other people could have done, or should have done, so that it could have turned out differently. I focus on what I should have already known so that I could have effected change in the situation. When I am done with that, I go right to blaming God for the issue. I think this style of response is linked to the pattern of abuse I endured growing up. I was treated as if I didn't know anything, yet was expected to already know everything. I believe this helped influence how I respond to loss and to things going wrong. We will explore the need to process these types of emotions and issues with God in Chapter Twelve.

You may respond differently. You may lean more toward negotiating with God to change things, offering something in return for your request, such as your devotion to Him or some type of service. There are endless variations of this theme. God can handle whatever direction you go with this. Each one of us needs to work out our grief in the way that fits our personality.

Instead of just denial, I have found that the bargaining stage can also be used to establish guilt. As I mentioned, this can be linked to your own upbringing and issues. One of the reasons we try to establish guilt could be because the circumstances seem so unfair and unjust. You may blame others, blame yourself, or try to find reasons why there needs to be some type of punishment for what happened. There may be feelings like, "This isn't right, so someone must be wrong!" This is part of the emotional roller-coaster ride I was referring to. You may shift from sadness, guilt, shame, resentment, regret, anger, disappointment, excitement, loneliness, joy, fear, blame, or countless other emotions, over and over again.

Yes, it is unfair! There is nothing fair about loss. Remember, loss is not part of the kingdom. It is not something we will ever understand. I don't think it will ever feel just and fair.

Even though reviewing your loss and trying to restructure what happened are common experiences in the grieving process, they are not very productive. I recommend returning to reality as soon as you can. Getting stuck in this aspect of the grieving process can cause you to obsess and not move forward. It can damage relationships and cause additional and unnecessary pain.

Another common experience with this aspect of the process are thoughts that you personally have done something wrong. Along with the trauma of the loss, the grief, depression, and the loneliness, a feeling of guilt can also start to grip you. Not only can you get a false sense that you are responsible for the loss, you can also have thoughts that you are processing it wrong, or somehow not quite handling your grieving appropriately.

I remember after our home burned, I walked around with an internal sense that I was doing something wrong. I couldn't even find words for it. It was a weird experience that I think connected to just how wrong the whole experience was, and my inability to accept the loss at first. Remember, none of this has to make sense. So much of what we go through in grieving is not a rational thought process. I believe the feeling I was experiencing helped initiate some of the imaginations of what I could have done differently, or what I should have already known.

This aspect of the grieving process is a type of distraction that, if unchecked, could cause you to stay in a loop of possibilities that can steal the life that is available. This can contribute to an attitude of unforgiveness, resentment, and anger that overtakes the process of freedom, peace, and joy being restored in your life. If you find yourself continuing to loop through this aspect of the process without resolution, I recommend pursuing help from someone who is qualified.

Forgiveness for the things you come up with in this process is vital to your ability to move on. They could be legitimate mistakes made or imagined possibilities. Either way, if you don't let go of these, your forward momentum can be stunted. If you need help with forgiveness, Chapter Seven of my book *Identity Restoration* will help you understand what forgiveness is and how to truly do it.

There are many things that *could* have or *should* have been done differently. If it could be done over, there are things that *would* be done in a different way. The problem is, it can't be done over, and replaying all the options will just continue to cause pain. The never-ending comparison of your current situation to different fantasy outcomes can keep you in a loop where you repeatedly experience the loss.

I have worked with many clients over the years who were stuck in a perpetual loop from a traumatic event in their lives. A belief system was established in that loop, causing an inability to break free from the trauma. Regardless of what was presently happening in their lives, there was an undercurrent of loss, pain, or trauma happening all the time. This is avoidable and healable through God revealing truth and giving your heart a choice.

Each time you let go of one of these imagined possibilities, it is a step toward the acceptance of your new normal. This will allow you to move forward. A very helpful tool in this process is to pay attention to your thoughts and feelings as you engage and disengage from these outcomes. This will allow you to work through your thoughts and help you decide how you want to live your life now.

You are not doing something wrong if you are engaging in these alternative, imagined outcomes. I believe these are not just a type of denial. I think they are also a way we are subconsciously trying to reconnect with who, or what, we lost. The problem is, this never really allows us to reconnect.

As we let go of the different *shoulda, coulda, woulda* imaginative loops, we can face the hurt and pain from the loss and begin to reconnect in a healthy way. We can then transition from being emotionally connected through the painful emotions into a remembrance of all the good things that we loved. This will help us establish our new normal and allow us to have emotional connections that are fulfilling and life giving.

There is no correct way you *should* be doing this. There is no need to look at what you *could* be doing better, and there is no way you *would* be able to do something different to fix it all. Take your time, and process how you need to process. You can do this. You will eventually thrive again in your new normal and be able to remember all the things you loved.

CHAPTER SEVEN

THE IMPORTANCE OF VULNERABILITY

Vulnerability! Wow, do we really have to talk about that? Haven't we suffered enough? Isn't it bad enough that I must try and move on with my life after this traumatic loss? Now you want to talk about being vulnerable, which brings with it the possibility of getting even more hurt?!

Unfortunately, in many social circles, vulnerability is not something that is respected or safe. I can look back at my own life and see that there was almost a standing "Miranda rights" rule: anything I said could and would be used against me. Your childhood may not have been like that, but I am sure all of us have experienced this at some level. Key people you thought you could trust may have used your vulnerability against you to try and hurt you. This is a very sad aspect of a fallen world.

Vulnerability is a very misunderstood concept. Even though it may not be said directly, it is commonly treated as a weakness. Because of this, it isn't something that is easily chosen during the grieving process. Vulnerability is almost a dirty word. It can be viewed as something that is either too emotional or unimportant. Through our experience in life, we have been trained to not show weakness. If vulnerability is a weakness, we can't go there.

One of the misunderstandings about vulnerability revolves around emotional sensitivity. The thinking that vulnerability always means connecting with some emotionally sensitive area in your heart is not accurate. It can be that, but it is not always. Vulnerability does not necessarily have anything to do with emotional sensitivity. It is a much broader concept than being emotional. I think it has been reduced to this understanding because of the trauma, betrayal, and abuse that people have experienced in their lives.

Another misunderstanding about vulnerability is that it has to do with retelling traumatic events that have happened. Commonly, people will mentally replay what has happened to them, and then retell it to others. They will repeatedly explain details of old traumatic events, thinking this is vulnerability. Sharing details of past trauma is not necessarily vulnerability. Many people use the detailed traumatic stories as a self-protection, keeping themselves from being vulnerable and known.

For example, think about a building that is protected with a security perimeter. Imagine someone is walking you around, showing you the perimeter of the building. They show you the walls, fences, and guards. They explain to you how there have been attempted break-ins, or damage done from previous incidents. They tell you in detail what happened, and how they defended themselves against it. They may even tell you how they have built up their defenses in those areas in case another attack comes. They could repeatedly walk you around the building, showing you all the trauma and explain the details of what happened, in the past, and still never reveal to you what is inside the building. In this same way, someone can share in-depth details about past traumatic events in their life and never let themselves be known. This is not vulnerability.

Before we discuss vulnerability in our grieving process, let's look at what vulnerability is. We have already looked at some aspects of what vulnerability isn't. Now let's focus more on what it is.

In my opinion, vulnerability is the willingness to authentically present yourself without any self-protections. This covers all aspects of yourself: your dreams, hopes, ideas, beliefs, thoughts, desires, emotions, disappointments, fears, strengths, giftings, inspirations, joys, hurts, and pain. It is so much more than just connecting with emotionally sensitive areas of your heart.

Vulnerability is not about what has happened on the outside. Vulnerability is being honest about what is happening on the inside. This is where healing happens. Unfortunately, sometimes we do not have people in our lives with whom it is safe to be vulnerable. If you do not have someone in your life who you can be honest with, get professional help. Having someone who you can be fully honest and vulnerable with is priceless.

Why do we need to talk about vulnerability in the grieving process? Because it is pivotal in the rebuilding of relationships, mindsets, and attitudes. Vulnerability is vital to rebuilding a healthy life.

"My grace is sufficient for you, for my power is made perfect in weakness." – 2 Corinthians 12:9

I do not believe that vulnerability is a weakness. I personally think vulnerability is where we are the strongest. The areas where we won't let ourselves be vulnerable are the weaknesses. Those are the areas we self-protect. We don't need to protect the areas of strength. If we will be honest with ourselves, in those areas of weakness, where we think we can't be vulnerable, we can allow God's strength to be made perfect. We can become vulnerable and free.

Honesty with ourselves is a key piece to vulnerability. Being honest with ourselves is where it all starts. If we are not willing to acknowledge and process what is actually happening in our hearts and minds, we may move into fear, resentment, and bitterness, causing us to self-protect and lose connection with ourselves and others. Eventually this can lead to an emotional disconnection from ourselves where we deny what is happening and perform to the cultural expectations around us.

As believers, we may think it is inappropriate to have and/or express certain thoughts or emotions. The idea that we shouldn't have these thoughts and emotions can cause us to deny what we are experiencing. This then prevents us from being honest with ourselves and being vulnerable with God.

> We destroy arguments and every lofty opinion raised against the knowledge of God, and take every thought captive to obey Christ. – 2 Corinthians 10:5

Vulnerability is a key part of the grieving process. You have a choice to either be vulnerable with God, receive comfort from Him, and build new healthy beliefs and responses, or isolate yourself and build new lies and unhealthy self-protections. Your willingness to be honest and vulnerable with God and yourself will help you heal. Healing begins with being honest with yourself about what you are feeling and thinking.

These moments of vulnerability with God are the places where healing happens. When you can authentically present yourself to God, without any limitations or self-protections, He will comfort you and provide authentic healing. Once you can be vulnerable with yourself, and with God, you may soon feel safe enough to be vulnerable with others.

You can do this. It may take time for you to be able to be vulnerable. That is OK. God will still be there when you are ready.

If you find you need help with this process, consider an Identity Coaching session. These sessions are designed to help you get to know yourself and understand how you self-protect. You can find out more about them at www.faithbygrace.org/identity-coaching.

CHAPTER EIGHT

SENSITIVITY TO LOSS

After a traumatic loss in your life, you may begin to experience a greater sensitivity to other losses. This sensitivity can express itself in ways you may not expect.

Even when the initial shock and trauma from your loss wears off, there can be a hyper-awareness of other losses you have previously experienced, especially if those losses have not been resolved. It can even cause you to mourn old losses you thought you had already processed.

This sensitivity is not limited to your own experiences. You can also become sensitive to other people's losses, or other traumatic events that are happening around you. Sensitivity to any kind of loss is sometimes heightened after a traumatic loss.

As I have said before, none of this needs to make any rational sense. Unfortunately, this sensitivity can be very distracting. It can almost feel like a setback in your grieving process. It is not a setback. It is just another aspect of the grieving process.

I personally experienced this in several ways after we lost our home. One of those ways was an increased sadness when I would hear about other traumatic events. Three months after the Carr Fire took our home, we had returned to Redding and were trying to reestablish a sense of normalcy in our lives. Right at this time, another tragic fire hit in Paradise, California, just south of Redding. This was beyond my ability to process at the time, and I went back into a sense of denial about that fire. Redding was still recovering from being evacuated, and now people from this new fire were coming here for relief and safety. I prayed for all involved when it came to mind, but I could not let myself even read about that fire for a while. I was not emotionally ready to process this new trauma right away. It was overwhelming to even think about. It took time before I could process any trauma that was happening around me. There was more work that was needed in my own trauma, before I could process a new one.

An additional way I experienced this was with having a hypersensitivity to other people's need for grace, due to what they might be going through, with no capacity to have grace for any of their unhealthy behavior. It was a weird experience of feeling a heightened sense of compassion for those around me and selfish judgementalism all at the same time. Thankfully I was aware of the sensitivity, so I was able to manage my own responses in those interactions. It wasn't always easy, and it often felt very unstable.

Another aspect of the sensitivity that I experienced was that I would randomly get triggered into feelings of an old loss that I had forgotten about. Sometimes, when I would remember something, it would just be a simple disruption. Other times, I would experience considerable grief when I remembered what I had lost. This was very frustrating and not enjoyable.

You may experience sensitivities like these, or in other ways I have not mentioned. The sensitivity you encounter will be unique to you, your losses, and your experiences. Allow yourself to process through your grief in the way you need.

There may even be a time of delay before you can face the different losses that get triggered. That is OK. Take the time you need. I do recommend intentionally returning to the issues. When you can, let yourself feel your feelings and process your thoughts about those losses. Stuffing the emotions and trying to deny them will not help. Your willingness to face these will determine whether you continue to stay in the loop of pain and sensitivity or begin to move forward.

Leaving the issues unresolved can lead to unhealthy responses to our grief. The most common unhealthy response to unresolved grief I have seen with my clients is an attempt to control and protect the variables in their lives. This control leads to a limitation of experiences, opportunities, relationships, and hope. Little by little, limitation and control eat away at the abundance of life that is available after the loss. The freedom, peace, and joy that is possible in the new normal becomes beyond reach. This doesn't have to be the case.

A willingness to be vulnerable with God about these sensitivities will allow you to process your thoughts and emotions in a way that can bring peace to your mind and your heart. It will not bring back your old life. Remember, you will never be the same again, and your life will never be the same again. Letting God meet you in the sensitive areas of your loss will help you establish a new normal where you can thrive again.

When you can take the time, let yourself experience God's presence in those sensitivities and allow Him to minister to you. You may not be ready for that yet, and that is OK. God is ready and willing to meet you whenever your heart is ready.

CHAPTER NINE

THE VALUE OF YOUR LOSS

The value of the loss of a relationship is priceless. I think it may be beyond my ability to comprehend or put a value on the loss of someone we love. In my opinion, it is too great to even attempt. I don't personally think we could even quantify the full value of the loss of a family member or a loved one. I will not be attempting to explore the concept of this value. At some point in our lives, we will all experience this unquantifiable loss.

It seems that most people understand and accept the need to grieve the value of a relationship or a life that is lost. There doesn't seem to be the same kind of understanding when it comes to the loss of material things. In this chapter, we are going to explore the value of material losses.

If you are willing, take a moment and let yourself think about an item you have that reminds you of a cherished memory or relationship. Go ahead, this is not a test. Just let yourself enjoy the way that makes you feel. Let yourself re-experience the emotions this item inspires that connect to the memory or relationship it reminds you of.

All of us have these items we hold on to. Even the most stoic of us hold on to something. What I have found is that even though we may know we have some items we are emotionally attached to, we don't really consider how sentimental we are, and just how many of those items we have. I myself didn't realize how many I had, until I lost them all. I was surprised at how nostalgic I am.

I bet you would be amazed if you took inventory of your belongings and thought about the relational connection to each one of them.

I have experienced something rather odd in religious circles. It's the thought process that infers that material items are meaningless. I've heard the insinuation that somehow it is not "Christian" to care about or value material things. I was stunned by this when I lost my home in the Northern California Carr Fire. People would try to encourage me and minimize my pain and grief by devaluing what I lost.

I heard things like:

"It was only material things you lost, at least you are okay."

"I know you don't care about material things."

"The only thing that matters is that you are okay."

"It's just stuff. You can replace all of it."

People would try to encourage me with the idea that since they knew I was a mature Christian, they knew I didn't care about the things I lost. This was odd to me because I definitely did care about what was lost, and I didn't see a conflict in that with my faith in Christ. We will explore this topic a little more in Chapter Eleven.

While I was still grieving the loss of my "stuff," I was talking with someone whose relative lost their home as well. I shared my condolences and they said, "He is okay, he is a Christian and doesn't care about material things." Wow! I was shocked. Could someone really think that not being emotionally affected by the loss of your home is somehow a Christian value? Could it be somehow less Christian to care about material things? That was one of those pivotal moments I will probably never forget. I believe this kind of mindset contributes to the unhealthy pattern of cognitive dissonance that I have witnessed in the lives of so many believers who are trying to deny their actual thoughts and perform and behave to cultural expectations.

We are not robots. We are emotional and relational beings. Having and valuing material things is not un-Christian! If the Lord created it, it has value. God even established a pattern of using material items as memorial stones of His goodness. In Exodus and Joshua, the Lord demonstrates this concept.

> ...So these stones shall be to the people of Israel a memorial forever. – Joshua 4:7

When I lost my home, I lost very valuable memorials that represented important relationships and events in my life. The value is not in the financial cost, it is in the relational and emotional connection. Created things carry value and meaning. We can look at all of God's creation and see value. You can see value in the specific details the Lord gave in the construction of the mercy seat, the ark of the covenant, or the temple. If there was no value in these material things, I don't think the Lord would have described them in such detail.

There is not something wrong with you, or your faith, because you value things you have. The fact that you care about your belongings does not make them false idols. It is not demonic worship to value a created thing. I think we need to have an understanding about the difference between financial cost and value. Yes, we can replace an item, or the financial cost of an item, but we can't always replace the true value of that item.

One of the items of mine that was just "stuff" that burned in the fire, was my grandmother's Bible. It was an old, old book that I remember seeing on her nightstand as a kid. It had all her handwritten notes and personal revelations written in it from years of study. It was also filled with old palm leaves she had collected from many Palm Sunday services. That Bible was an intimate connection to my grandmother, my faith, and some of the very few good memories I have of my childhood. Yes, I can buy a new Bible, but I can never replace the true value of that book. This reality is painful and was one of the unexpected punches in the gut I experienced when I remembered this treasured memorial for the first time after the fire. The value was not in the material of the book. It was in the memories, connections, and love that it reminded me of.

It is possible to get our values misplaced. If you ever wonder if your value for something has crossed over into an unhealthy place, check to see if you value it above your relationship with God or people. Most of us do not fall in that category. If you find that you do value things above relationships, you can be healed of that too! This would just be another opportunity to be vulnerable and honest with God so you can experience His grace and redemption.

Unfortunately, this idea that it is not Christian to value material things can cause us to deny our loss. Ignoring or devaluing the loss we experienced will keep us from being able to grieve and move forward. This type of denial can cause us to move into judgment and condemnation for the feelings we have about what we lost. This can cause us to add additional pain and grief that will linger unresolved and keep us from moving forward. Accepting the loss of the actual value we feel and perceive and allowing God to meet us in it, without judging what we should or should not feel, will help us move forward and find peace.

The items you display or keepsakes you store have meaning to you. They are important because they serve you in that way. Will you be okay without them? Yes. Are there things that are of more value, such as the life and health of you and your family? Absolutely! However, loss is real and tangible, no matter how big or small. It doesn't need to be compared to a perceived greater loss.

It is okay, and even necessary, to acknowledge the loss of important and meaningful items, so that you can move on in peace. Minimizing the value of your loss only keeps you in denial of the pain. This won't move you forward in a healthy way.

You have permission to grieve the loss of "stuff" you may have lost.

If you are willing, take a few moments today in a quiet place. Let your mind go to something you have lost that you haven't fully acknowledged or grieved. Allow yourself to admit, without judgment or condemnation, that you did care about what was lost, and that losing it hurt (made you sad, didn't seem fair, caused you pain). Let yourself experience and process your emotions. Ask God to comfort you in your grief; allow His kindness to minister to you. When you're ready, allow your heart to let go of any hurt and let peace take the place of the pain.

CHAPTER TEN

COMPARISON TRAP

H ave you ever thought "I should be grateful about my loss because ...," or "I shouldn't feel bad about my loss because ...?" Unfortunately, this is a very common and very unhelpful tool that usually just adds guilt and condemnation to your grief.

Think about this for a minute. Imagine a situation in your life, maybe as a child, when you had to eat a particular food that you really didn't like or want. Now, if I told you that you should be grateful for what you have been given to eat, even though you don't like it, what comes to mind as the reason why you should be grateful? Pause and think about that for a moment. I am sure you have heard this at some point in your life. We should be grateful for what we have because someone else doesn't have it, or they have less. At some level, we have all been trained in this. This type of unhealthy thinking has even permeated how we look at loss.

Looking back, I can still remember specific times in my life when I would tell myself that I shouldn't be affected by my loss. One of those was when I was a child and my parents gave away our dog. I do not remember how old I was, but I was young. My bedroom was right next to the front room. One night when I was supposed to be sleeping, I heard my parents talking to their friends about our dog. Through the wall I could hear them giving our dog away. This was a surprise for me because they did not tell me anything about getting rid of our dog beforehand. We had never talked about this and it was shocking to me. I never even got to say goodbye. I went to sleep that night sad and confused. When I woke up the next morning, I realized it wasn't just a dream. Our dog was gone, and no one mentioned anything about it to me. I determined not to be affected by it. I never let my parents know it bothered me, and I wouldn't let myself be honest about it to myself either. I never mentioned anything to my parents, and I don't remember ever discussing that dog again. I shut it down at such an intensity that I still don't remember its name, and this memory is the only one I have of that dog. This was just one of the building blocks in the process of stuffing what I was feeling deep down inside and living an empty life of emotional stoicism.

I understand that what I just shared may not fit your situation. Each one of us has our own set of experiences and emotional responses. However, it seems that discounting loss for "whatever reason" is a common strategy. I really noticed this after we lost our home in the fire. As I mentioned in Chapter Nine, people would try to comfort me by comparing our situation to some greater loss that could have happened. I also encountered many people devaluing their own loss because they felt theirs was not as intense as ours. This is such a common practice; I don't think people realize they are doing it.

The intensity of someone else's loss does not negate the value of your own. Comparing your loss to someone else's with thoughts like, "I shouldn't feel bad about my loss because theirs was so much worse," is not helpful. It won't resolve your pain and can delay your grieving process. Imagining how your situation could have been worse and thinking, "I should just be grateful because this worse situation didn't happen," can devalue your loss and distract you from addressing your grief.

I have found that gratitude by comparison is never grateful. Trying to make ourselves grateful by comparing our situation to someone else's will not resolve the pain. There is not something wrong with you because you are sad about your loss. You are not ungrateful because you can't just be joyful in the middle of your grief. Allowing yourself to address the real loss, without comparing, devaluing, or denying the value of it, will allow you to grieve through your loss and find peace, joy, and gratitude for what you do have. God gave us the grieving process so that we can reset to this new normal we were never intended to experience in the first place. Give yourself permission to face the loss, grieve, and acknowledge the true value of what you lost.

There are two significant problems with using comparison as a coping mechanism. First, it keeps you from being present in reality. Comparison is a type of denial that disconnects you from your actual loss. This form of denial will cause you to move into a false reality where your loss is somehow good because it is not as bad as this other worse situation. The problem with this is that it keeps you from being able to process the grief of your real loss. Second, it opens up the whole scope of possibilities, not just the worse. When you compare, it will naturally cause your mind to explore the worse as well as the better. This opens the potential of adding bitterness, jealousy, and frustration to your already painful situation. These two problems can keep you in a loop of comparison instead of staying present in your grief and being able to process your thoughts and emotions about your actual loss. This will add extra stress, pain, and hurt to an already difficult process.

Not allowing yourself to process the sadness, pain, and grief of your loss can lead to additional internal and external problems in your life. This can include depression, unproductiveness, anxiety, sickness, hopelessness, career dissatisfaction, relational disconnection, addiction, or divorce, just to name a few. I can personally see how it contributed to procrastination in my own life. This caused me to not address issues in my life because I wouldn't let myself be affected by the emotions. This created a pattern of not being passionate about my relationships, desires, goals, or dreams; I allowed them to just fade away. Sadly, I can look back and see many friendships I had with wonderful people in my life that just disappeared because of my apathy. Close relationships were difficult and limited.

Along with having limited relationships, I wouldn't really let myself dream either. If I did have a dream, I wouldn't let myself get excited about the possibility. I would try to protect myself from disappointment by not letting myself hope and dream. I can now see that this type of thinking caused me to live in a perpetual lifestyle of the disappointment I was trying to avoid. All of this also caused me to not take steps to pursue a career, delaying stability in my life. Additionally, this led me into a lifestyle of denying what was actually happening and pretending like everything was OK. If I was affected emotionally by anything, I would make myself feel guilty for having these feelings. I was so trained to believe that these emotions were a weakness that I would also shame myself for being so weak. Yes, it was as miserable as it sounds.

The intensity of your grieving will not last forever. It may seem impossible to ever be happy again, but it is possible. If you allow yourself to address your actual loss, you will eventually feel better. It is OK if you are not OK right now. If you are finding yourself stuck in your grief, or unable to acknowledge it, I recommend getting help outside of yourself. A simple tool I have recommended to hundreds of my clients is *Good Grief* by Granger Westburg. Another great option would be to find a grief counselor near you or sign up for an Identity Coaching session at www.faithbygrace.org. You are worth investing into, and freedom is available.

Comparing your loss to others will not help you heal. Your loss is real, and you have permission to grieve.

CHAPTER ELEVEN

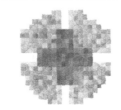

BAD ADVICE

We have looked at some of the aspects of the grieving process that are happening internally. In this chapter we are going to look at part of the grieving process that may be happening externally.

One of the unfortunate aspects of the grieving process that you must get through is the bad advice, unhelpful encouragement, and misdirected comfort you will receive. This will require a grace and patience that may sometimes be difficult for you, due to being in the aftermath of a traumatic loss.

While going through this, it is helpful to remember that none of us understand loss or really know how to respond properly in the moment. I have been studying grief for a while now, and I am always uncomfortable and unsure how to respond to someone who has just experienced loss. This is difficult for everyone. I believe everyone around us is doing the best they can in this awkward, confusing time. I also think it is helpful to realize that, for the most part, people have good intentions while they are giving you bad advice, unhelpful encouragement, or misdirected comfort.

People want to help. The empathy and compassion they have for you will be activated, and they will try to help you in some way. Even though there will be plenty of good advice, helpful encouragement, and soothing comfort, some will not know how to help, and they will offer all types of unwanted attempts at helping. It is very important to have people around you who you can trust and with whom you can be vulnerable. If you do not have that type of community available, I recommend finding a therapist or grief group.

Let's look at these three different experiences separately.

BAD ADVICE

You will have plenty of unrequested advice coming your way after a loss. Some of it will be very helpful, and some of it will not.

For some reason, it seems we have a natural inclination to help fix things. Some of us find it difficult to just listen and have compassion. Some will move into "fix it" mode. After we have experienced a loss, some of the people in our lives may try to fix it. There can be many different motives for this. It could be because of their love for us, their tendency toward codependency, their simple need to fix things, their own unresolved grief, or the awkwardness of not knowing what to do or how to relate to us after a loss. People won't always know how to respond, but they sometimes feel like they must. Most people are simply trying to find a way to ease your pain.

The advice we receive will usually be about what we should or shouldn't do. Sometimes this can be tough to discern because, like I said, some advice will be good, and some will be bad. This can be difficult to sort through, especially considering that we may be in a potentially fluctuating mental and emotional state. We may be unable to think clearly because of the fog or feel like we are spinning out of control because of the wheel of emotions.

Considering you are reading my book, I will assume it is OK to give you my advice. I recommend delaying any major decisions that do not need to be made right away. Have trusted, wise counsel around you who can help with the decisions that have to be made. You may be tempted to isolate yourself. As much as you can, let others help you. As you come out of the fog and begin to live life outside of the trauma bubble, you can review those decisions that you didn't need to make right away.

During this time of grief, you are still who you are in Christ. You still have the mind of Christ and have access to the Spirit of wisdom and revelation (Ephesians 1:17). As we process through the grief and continue to reconnect with who we are, we will have greater access to this wisdom and revelation. This is an interesting time of believing in yourself, still trusting yourself, and allowing yourself to submit to healthy guidance and advice.

UNHELPFUL ENCOURAGEMENT

One of the most common unhelpful things I experienced after the loss of my home was when people would try to encourage me out of my grief to make me feel better. This was never something that was enjoyable for me. It always made it more uncomfortable and awkward in the moment. It was difficult to figure out how to respond in the conversation because it was so disconnected from the reality I was experiencing.

You can expect this to happen. People will try to encourage you to "look on the bright side," or "be grateful because at least it wasn't worse," or you should "be thankful because of _____." Some will try to encourage you out of your grief because of their own discomfort with loss, as well as their inability to be present in the moment with you. Loss and grief are awkward, and people don't know what to do with them. Because of this, they will try to encourage someone out of the grief and into some type of happiness. The problem with this kind of unhelpful encouragement is that it can make someone who is grieving feel like they are doing something wrong because they can't just be grateful and happy. Remember from Chapter Ten, there is not something wrong with you because you are sad about your loss. You are not ungrateful because you can't just be joyful in the middle of your grief.

The Scripture does not say, "Encourage those who weep or mourn." It does not say, "Rejoice with those who weep or mourn." It says to weep with those who weep; mourn with those who mourn. Not everyone will be in an emotionally healthy place where they can do this with you. Please know, there is not something wrong with you because you need people to mourn and weep with you in your loss. You do not need to be encouraged out of your grief and mourning. In time, as you intentionally stay present in your thoughts and emotions, and process your grief, you will find encouragement in the Lord.

Even though there is no need to be encouraged out of your grief, there are ways to be encouraged and built up in your grief. I am sure you have experienced people who have been there for you and were encouraging you while you were mourning. If you do not have healthy people around you who are letting you know that you are OK, that you are not doing anything wrong, and that you are allowed to feel and grieve, I recommend finding help through a group or counselor.

MISDIRECTED COMFORT

My first major experience of loss was when my dad died. He was diagnosed with non-Hodgkin lymphoma when I was in high school. I did not understand the severity of this at the time, and I did not realize the impact this had on me. I can look back now and see how I found ways to numb myself and ignore the reality of what was happening. He went through a pretty aggressive chemotherapy treatment and the cancer went into remission. He lived another twelve years before it came back. I had just come to faith shortly before we found out his cancer had returned. I still remember the moment driving my dad home from the doctor appointment when he told me the cancer was back. It was a very weird slow-motion experience that I don't have words for. He tried to nonchalantly tell me that the cancer was back, but I felt the weight of his words and we were both in shock because of the trauma of this painful reality. We drove the rest of the way home, unable to speak.

That moment is imprinted in my mind and my memory. It kicked off a very painful and emotional time of grief for me. Growing up, I did not have a close relationship with my dad. Now that I was an adult, we were growing closer and getting to know each other. The hope I had for this father/son relationship had now been taken. There were several times when I would break down and sob because of the grief. Breaking down like this was an unusual experience for me because of the lack of vulnerability and expression of emotion I experienced in my youth. I spun out through several stages of grief and loss while building up to his death, all the while trying to hold on to hope and faith for a miracle. If I remember it correctly, the process before he died was worse than his death. I talk about this concept in Chapter Fourteen, Impending Loss. After he died, there was an odd sense of relief for him because he was no longer being tortured with the cancer. This relief seemed to help me through some of the grief of losing him.

After my dad's death, I was introduced to the awkwardness of having to interact with people who seemed to think they were comforting me, even though they weren't. It is a surreal experience that is not comforting at all, when people come up to you needing to be comforted because of your loss. You may have experienced something like this yourself, and possibly not even understood what was happening. I have found people can respond to someone else's loss in a way that misdirects the need for comfort to be for themselves, instead of the person who just experienced a loss.

Death and loss are very uncomfortable for people. We have looked at some of the reasons for this. We were not created to experience loss. We don't understand it and I don't think we ever will. Loss is awkward, uncomfortable, and confusing for everybody, not just you. I have never felt fully confident and comfortable engaging with someone who is grieving. It is still a struggle for me. I believe the Lord gave us the grieving process so we can somehow reestablish a sense of normalcy in our lives. If we are willing to face our loss and process our grief, we will be able to be comforted, and eventually comfort others.

When someone has not processed their own loss, they can retrigger into the unresolved pain and grief and be extra sensitive to someone else's loss. In this sensitivity, they will unknowingly misdirect the need for comfort to be for themselves when they are engaging with you in your loss. Sometimes people believe that if they don't express the depths of their own emotions to you, that you won't think they care enough. There is a place for them to share their pain, but it is best if they hold off until you have had the freedom to express your own.

Like I had mentioned in the beginning, you will experience these different aspects of interaction with others, and you may find it difficult. You will need to learn how to maneuver through this and let yourself communicate your boundaries and needs. Some of the unhelpful interactions you will ignore, and some you will engage with. You can do this. Remember, it is OK that you are not enjoying and do not appreciate the bad advice, unhelpful encouragement, and misdirected comfort. As much as you can, let the Lord meet you in these awkward times, learn from them, and allow yourself to be in the grieving process where you are. Remember that those around you care, and want to help you, even if they stumble in their attempts at first. Remember that you do not need to be different or try to make yourself be happy. You need to grieve, and you have permission to be real in your grief. You are going to get through this.

CHAPTER TWELVE

GRIEVING THE LOSS OF A GOOD GOD

This is a very sensitive topic. I am aware that even touching this subject may give an opportunity for religious criticism and judgment. It is sometimes difficult for us to be honest about our feelings of disappointment with God. In this chapter, I hope to help you meet with God in any deep, wounded areas of disappointment and loss so that you can experience freedom.

A few years ago, we endured one of the toughest financial struggles of our lives. We led a ministry in Maryland until we moved to California in 2013. For several different reasons, after moving to California, we slowly lost some of our ministry support. Sadly, we also lost some relationships with close friends during this time. This was a very painful season that challenged my faith in many ways. We were transitioning how our ministry operated, and we were having trouble recovering from the financial shift. After struggling like this for a few years, it was becoming difficult to manage emotionally and financially.

While wrestling with these financial and relational losses, we also had to prepare for our son leaving for college. I was excited for him but very sad about the distance that would be between us. He was going to college in Southern California about ten hours away. This was the first time our family was going to be separated, and it added to the emotional and financial stress I was already experiencing. I still remember standing in his room after he had packed up all his belongings. I could feel the sadness and emptiness inside of me that was represented by that empty room.

The day we packed up the van and left to take him to college was a significant internal battle for me. We had no money in our personal account, no money in our ministry account, and no credit available. I had no idea how this was all going to work out. I was trying to stay hopeful, but I felt helpless and unsupported by God. Thankfully, we had some leftover hotel reward points from past travel that allowed us to work out the hotel stay for the trip. We knew we could get him there, and we had a place to stay, so we loaded up our van and set off for his university.

This was a difficult trip. Our son was heading off to college, and we wanted to be able to provide everything for him. This landmark event that is supposed to be a fun and exciting time seemed to be getting stolen from me. The helplessness I felt was building. I did my best to stay positive and not let him know, but I am sure he knew something was going on. I was not only experiencing the emotional separation of our son leaving for college, but also the financial uncertainty of how it would happen. This was really rough! To be honest, at the time I had no sense of security for the Lord providing for us.

While on our trip heading south, a dear friend called me and let me know that they had been inspired by God to give to our ministry. This was a beautiful reminder of God's goodness in the middle of a tough time, and it allowed us to take a partial paycheck. In ministry, you get a paycheck if there is money in the ministry account. Sometimes it is a short check, and you hopefully recover later. Every month is an act of faith. We have been doing this since 2001, so we are somewhat used to it, but after several years of juggling low finances, it had become difficult.

The surprise donation from our friend was a beautiful blessing in the midst of a stressful time. But since we had been through an unusually tough few years of financial struggles, I was finding it a battle to stay positive. This surprise really helped, but I had received one too many financial punches, and it had knocked the wind out of me. My faith was beat down. Despite the sadness of our son moving away, my wife was able to pray and receive encouragement from the Lord. She was in a better place emotionally than I was. I had been trying to hide my state of despair, and our real financial position from her, because I didn't want to bring her down. I know how ridiculous that sounds, but it seemed like a good idea at the time. She is extremely gifted in discernment, so she was actually aware the whole time.

After getting our son settled in his new apartment, we stayed with some friends in the area for a few days. The drive to our friend's house was an emotional time. Driving away from our son's new apartment and leaving him there was not easy. I tried to hold it together, but I began to cry as Kathryn and I talked about the transition. Kathryn and I cried as we tried to comfort and encourage each other on the way. One afternoon, when we were alone, it all seemed to come to a head. Kathryn asked me what was wrong. I had tried to just blow it off, but she pressed in. At one point when she asked me what was really happening,

I told her I was just grieving. Then she asked me what I was grieving. Up to that point, I don't even think I knew. I could have just hidden behind the grief of our son moving away, but there was more to it. What came out of my mouth after that was, "I am grieving the loss of a good God." OK, so there it was. Wow, I was even somewhat taken back by it myself. I obviously had some issues I needed to work out with God.

Just to be clear, I know God is good! It is His nature. I know this—I just don't always *believe* this. We have been intentionally exploring vulnerability and honesty throughout this book. Being honest with ourselves and with God to directly confront the beliefs that do not line up with the truth is critical to the process of healing. We have all had experiences that make us question the goodness of God. We can even read accounts of many of the characters in the Scriptures expressing their real thoughts and feelings to God. From Job and David in the Old Testament, all the way to Peter denying Jesus, out of fear, in the New Testament. God is not afraid of our real thoughts and feelings. There is no reason for us to be afraid of them either.

As we have discussed throughout this book, loss is never going to make sense. We were not created to experience loss, and when we do it is traumatic. This trauma and confusion make it difficult to understand how a good God could allow these things to happen. These are legitimate thoughts that need to be processed with God. Sadly, I have worked with so many people who are still suffering from an old loss because they were not able to address their real thoughts and feelings. Often, I experience well-meaning believers denying their pain and real beliefs, while telling themselves they *know* God is good. I believe this is where a lot of the bad advice, discussed in Chapter Eleven, comes from. The denial of our real thoughts and feelings, in our attempt to fit a religious expectation, will not help us heal.

The willingness to confront any beliefs that God is not good will allow us to process and be free of them. Yes, absolutely, there are things that happen that are horrific and beyond understanding. I do not understand the fullness of how God's sovereignty, free will, sin, redemption, good, and evil all play out in this fallen world. I do know God will meet you in your misery, where you may be disappointed in Him, blaming Him, or even hating Him for the loss you have experienced. Don't be afraid to go there. There is no lie you believe about God that He doesn't already know and hasn't already taken to the cross for you.

We have all experienced loss and disappointment. Many of my coaching clients have experienced unimaginably tragic losses that hit at the core of their being. Religious platitudes and distractions never seemed to help them. These only seemed to prolong their pain and often caused them to pull away from their relationship with God. Regardless of how traumatic our losses have been, it is important to process any thoughts or feelings we have about God in the midst of it all.

One of the reasons I was able to work through my issues with God about finances was because I was willing to be honest about them. Confronting these issues allowed me to go deeper into some of the provision issues from my childhood. It was these issues that had shaped unhealthy perspectives about God's nature and inspired the helplessness and insecurity I was experiencing.

I have learned not to pretend with God. It is unproductive to give a religious performance of praise while harboring bitterness in our hearts. Just as my wife knew there was something deeper going on with me, God knew exactly what I was thinking and feeling. Being honest with Him about my struggle was the best thing I could do for my relationship with Him. Once I was honest with God about the lies I was believing, I was able to allow His love in and receive comfort for my pain.

Don't get the wrong idea. I am not saying I was magically fixed of all my financial issues and lived happily ever after. It has been a journey of revelation, healing, struggling, doubting, hoping, stumbling, and getting back up. Our journeys of grieving, healing, and faith are not always pretty. You will stumble in your grieving process. The Word tells us that we all stumble in many ways. Although we will stumble, the Lord is always available to help us.

Now to Him who is able to keep you from stumbling and to present you blameless before the presence of His glory with great joy, to the only God, our Savior, through Jesus Christ our Lord, be glory, majesty, dominion, and authority, before all time and now and forever. Amen. – Jude 24-25

Not only is He there to help us get back up when we stumble, He is always there comforting us and guiding us so we can keep from stumbling. Sometimes we receive the help to not stumble. Sometimes we will stumble and receive His help to get back up. Either way, you can do this. You have what it takes to be honest, face your thoughts and feelings, confront your pain, and bring it all to the Lord.

Thankfully, God is loving, gracious, and merciful to work with us through the grief of any loss, perceived or real. It is safe to allow Him into those deep, sad, wounded areas of our soul, even in those places we are most afraid of going because we may not fully believe in His goodness. Jesus paid for it all, and there is no need for us to continue in our private suffering. Sometimes it is difficult for us to go there on our own. If you are unable to go there on your own, it is OK. You are allowed to be honest and need help.

CHAPTER THIRTEEN

ABSTRACT LOSS

Not every loss we experience is tangible. Some losses are abstract or even just perceived. It doesn't have to be a huge traumatic event that initiates a sense of loss and causes the need to grieve. In this chapter, I intend to help you acknowledge, grieve, and heal from those intangible losses.

You may have been dreaming of or hoping for something for a long time. You may have been planning and preparing for a family, a relationship, a career, an event, a degree, a purchase, or even an adventure, and now it is unattainable. Losses like these are real, even though they are not as tangible as others. I have worked with many clients who were experiencing sadness without knowing why. When we would explore the reasons for the sadness, we would sometimes find the loss of a hope or dream. Often, this would even surprise the person because they had discounted the idea of being bothered by such an intangible issue. Since they had never processed it, the sadness and grief were still there unresolved.

Years ago, while working with some of my coaching clients, I noticed that after they received healing and freedom, they began to grieve. This was an interesting phenomenon that I did not understand at first. What I discovered is that people will see more clearly once they are set free from old, dysfunctional relational patterns. Once they can see the relationship for what it really is, they may need to grieve the loss of what they had perceived the relationship to be. This is an interesting set of circumstances that not everyone experiences, but many do. Having to let go of something you only *thought* you had, that you didn't really have, can be confusing and painful. Sometimes additional coaching was needed to help them get through the different dynamics of the relational shift. When this type of healing occurs, grieving is an important part of their healing process.

This was not the only abstract pattern of loss I noticed with my clients. I also found that sometimes when people received healing from more intricate and sophisticated self-protections, there would also be a need for grieving. Our systems of self-protection can become so familiar and comfortable that there can be a sense of loss after healing. It is almost like they became a trusted friend we had been relying on. There can even be an experience of loneliness as we recalibrate to our new life without this self-protection. If you need or want more information about how we use self-protections, my book *Identity Restoration* explains this topic.

I realize it is an odd concept that someone may need to grieve after receiving freedom and healing, but this is a real experience for some. Even in a good situation, like healing, there can be a need to let yourself grieve something you've lost. Remember, your loss doesn't have to be tangible in order to warrant the need for grieving.

I have found there can even be a need to grieve something that you only perceived you had. Our perceptions are our reality. When we lose something very meaningful to us, something we only perceived we had, it can be a real loss. Experiencing this significant reality shift can be very jarring to us emotionally and can initiate a need to recalibrate and adapt to a new normal. The grieving process allows us to adapt to this new normal.

I personally experienced an abstract loss when my mother died. She was a person with whom it was very difficult to be in a relationship. When she died, there was an aspect of loss just from losing her physical presence. As dysfunctional as the relationship was, she was the mother I had known all my life. But the grief that impacted me the most was losing the chance of having a healthy relationship with a mom. The possibility of having a healthy mother/son relationship was now gone. There was no way to have that now. This grief snuck up on me and caught me by surprise. I didn't understand what was going on at first. I wasn't even aware I was hoping for this until it was taken away. My mother was also the last of my parental relatives to die. My father was the first to go, then my grandmother, then my mom. Those were the only parental figures I had growing up. I never knew any of my other grandparents. This was not just the loss of the hope of a relationship with my mom, but the finality of any parental relationship. Even though this was abstract and intangible, it was a real loss that I had to process.

Confronting these abstract losses is important. In these losses, the enemy can sneak in lies like, "This shouldn't bother you," or, "This isn't important," or even something like, "Look what other people are dealing with." It is so easy to discount the need to process a loss that is intangible. It isn't even a "real" thing! The problem with discounting these losses is that it establishes a pattern of denial that may eventually be applied to the tangible losses as well. The pain and hurt from a loss you have experienced, but not processed, can keep you from grieving new losses. This grief can build up and eventually reach a breaking point that will cause collateral damage to your life and your relationships. By courageously admitting and confronting your losses, you can process your grief, and experience the freedom and peace that are available in your new normal.

Unfortunately, we don't always receive grace from others for this type of grief. Often others who don't understand grief, or who deny their own grief, will try to tell us there is no need to grieve. Many of my clients have experienced shame and ridicule for being affected by experiences in their lives. The enemy may even use trusted people in your life to accuse you of things like, "You are too sensitive," or "There is something wrong with you," for acknowledging your pain. Confronting your pain and being honest about your feelings is not being overly sensitive, it is being brave.

As we are acknowledging our losses and confronting them, it is good to be aware of the unhealthy possibility of making our loss an identity. If this happens, we can get stuck in the loss and find ourselves unable to move forward. We will explore this in Chapter Eighteen. Even though loss can be excruciatingly painful, you are still more than what you have lost. If you find yourself unable to move forward in your process and are overwhelmed by your loss, I recommend seeking professional help.

Please understand, I am not trying to promote the idea of looking for things to grieve. If you are experiencing freedom, peace, and joy, keep experiencing those! But if you are not, and you have been through some type of loss, then I recommend confronting these painful emotions by allowing yourself to process your grief. Denying your sadness, pain, and grief will never help you. Denial will never resolve your pain. It will only cause the pain and grief to be redirected and expressed in some unhelpful way. Believe me, it is easier to confront these losses now, rather than letting them build up and cause collateral damage.

If you seem to be experiencing any unexplained sadness and grief, take a moment to ask God if there are any losses that you haven't acknowledged or let yourself grieve. If so, give yourself permission to acknowledge the loss, process any emotions that come up, forgive as needed, and receive comfort from God. Give yourself the time you need to recover. Self-care is an essential part of a healthy life. Take your time, remind yourself of His promises, and let your heart be encouraged.

Freedom is available, and you can do this! Many people believe in you and are willing to help you.

CHAPTER FOURTEEN

IMPENDING LOSS

Sometimes loss doesn't take us by surprise. Sometimes it is a slow, painful process as we wait for the conclusion of what we know is coming.

We could be experiencing the harsh journey of a terminal illness with a loved one, preparing for a move away from a loving community, walking through a failing relationship, or living through the last years with elderly family members. These are just a few examples of how we lose something very dear to us in a gradual process. Instead of one big loss, we experience a slow, piece-by-piece loss as we grieve the different aspects of what we are losing.

This type of loss is not uncommon. We are experiencing this all the time. As we grow, change, follow our dreams, and pursue our own path in life, we are continually losing some aspects of our relationships, experiences, comforts, friends, and family. Little by little we have developed a capacity for the smaller, less impactful losses in our lives. The bigger ones are usually the ones we remember and have trouble with.

I have personally experienced this process several times in my life. The first one I remember is preparing to move from my childhood home because of new road construction. This new road plan went right through our yard and included the removal of our house. This carried the weird feeling of almost being erased from the neighborhood. I already had so many insecurities and feelings of rejection, this just added to it and confirmed it. It is still odd when I am in town and I drive by the empty lot that used to be my yard. There is just an empty field with some trees and bushes that I remember being in my yard. All the other homes are still there, with all the memories. But my childhood home is gone.

The toughest impending loss I can remember was when my father was dying of cancer. His original diagnosis came when I was still in high school. As I mentioned, I was about sixteen when we first found out. This was a difficult time for our family, and one that impacted many aspects of my life. Thankfully, after this treatment, his cancer went into remission.

The really tough time was when the cancer returned. For me, the last year of his life was a slow, painful dismantling of the different aspects of our relationship. As I mentioned in Chapter Eleven, now that I was an adult, we were building a better relationship. Little by little, in the last year of his life, there was less and less of my father present. We were no longer able to have coffee together in the morning. There were no more afternoons working together in the garden, no more projects he needed help with around the house, and no more times watching him give my daughter a flower while he let her steal his hat off his head. These are just a few of the different aspects of the slow, piece-by-piece dismantling of our relationship. My daughter was losing her Pop-Pop, my son would never get to know him, and I was losing my dad.

I did not fully understand what I was going through at that time. I can look back now and see what was happening. At the time, I mostly just survived the experience. It isn't uncommon for people to just survive the loss. How to handle loss is not something we are usually taught. It is something we each experience in our own way, and we develop our own methods of coping. Some of the methods are helpful, some are destructive.

You can experience all the different stages of the grieving process multiple times over as you slowly lose aspects of something, or someone, you care about. Sometimes, the anticipation of the final loss can be overwhelming as you are still trying to work through the aspects of loss you are already experiencing. The multiple emotional impacts can begin to bring confusion and throw you into the emotional roller-coaster ride of grief.

The confusion is only part of the problem. There are so many questions and so many thoughts that can run through your head—why, how, what, when? It is a unique experience to go through grieving an impending loss. Slowly losing the different dynamics of a relationship, a community, or a career will hit us in stages. You can have different aspects of the grieving process triggering off from the various dynamics of the loss, while still processing the impending loss. This can be an emotional and mental roller-coaster ride that you don't understand fully. After all, it makes sense that we will go through the stages of grief after a loss, but when combined with the process of grief that can happen before we have even experienced the final loss, it can be a lot to deal with.

It is very helpful to intentionally face the different aspects of loss as you experience them. Some people believe they need to be the strong one in the situation. Just remember, denial is not strength. Intentionally staying present in your emotions and processing what you are feeling is an important part of the healing process. It is OK to be strong for those who need you to be strong, but for your own benefit, and the benefit of others, take some time for yourself and process what you are experiencing. If you are going through this right now, it is OK.

If you can, slow down, take a breath, and let others help you. We can distract ourselves with all the different details that need to be taken care of for an impending loss. This can be problematic afterward when we no longer have all the things to distract ourselves. Not facing our real emotions can build up into a much bigger and worse situation, causing added emotional and relational pain. Sometimes it can even cause an emotional crash. If we are willing to process and grieve in real time, we will be able to be strong when needed. It does not help to ignore or distract ourselves from the grief. If we can stay present in our emotions and process the grief we are experiencing, it will help keep us from getting overwhelmed at the impending loss. It will be much easier if you let yourself be present in each aspect of the grief as you prepare yourself for the eventual outcome.

Sometimes, you may feel completely out of control, like you are just being pulled forward through a tunnel. The unknowns of what life will be like after the loss can be daunting. We can get lost in our imaginations about how terrible it will be afterward. This is another unhelpful distraction we sometimes use during an impending loss. I still remember a quote from an old pastor friend of mine. He told me, "God gives you grace for your situation, not your imagination." This has been a very helpful principle for me over the years. I have found it very helpful to stay mentally and emotionally present in my situation so that

I can access God's grace. Imagining the worst doesn't help us heal.

Most importantly, I want you to know that you aren't getting this wrong. We all deal with loss in the best way we can in any given moment. My goal is simply to encourage you, as much as you are able, to process in real time so that you can access the grace of God in the present moment. You don't have to steady your heart for an upcoming loss all by yourself. God will give you what you need from one moment to the next. You will get through this. If you find yourself struggling, please find someone to help. Don't be afraid to seek professional help as well. Getting help sorting through your thoughts and emotions while you prepare for an impending loss will be a tremendous benefit for you, and for those for whom you are trying to be strong.

CHAPTER FIFTEEN

THE FIRSTS ARE THE WORST

We have all had to experience life for the first time without. Without the person we love, the community we knew, our family, our home, our favorite possession, our job, or our familiar comforts. Loss can be challenging enough, but being reminded of it every time we have a new first experience can be miserable.

These first experiences after a loss can be triggering and extremely painful. We all have established cherished traditions that are significantly affected by our losses. It is almost unimaginable to experience holidays or special occasions without your loved one being there. It can also be difficult to experience traditions in a different location, that were always celebrated in a home you have lost. Even having to perform a menial task without the familiar surroundings or possessions you once had can be troublesome.

I still remember how impactful it was to just make coffee for the first time after we lost our home. We had been displaced and were living in a hotel for weeks after the fire. I didn't have to make coffee for myself that whole time. Once we were settled back into a temporary home and I made coffee for the first time, it triggered the grief of losing my morning traditions. The mornings were a very special time for me. I would wake up before everybody else in the house, make coffee, have time with the Lord, and work on whatever book I was writing at that time. I would sit on the back deck enjoying the mountain view and the California weather, along with a cup of coffee in one of my favorite mugs. It was glorious! All the different dynamics of that loss hit me the first time I made coffee after the fire. Some of my favorite mugs were ones that originally belonged to my dad. This first time making coffee triggered grief from multiple different relational and traditional dynamics that were now gone.

Just like my morning routines, sometimes we are not even aware of the sentimental attachment until it hits. We can suddenly be reminded of something we were not even remembering about our relationships or routines. The rituals we establish in our lives are almost subconscious; we don't always think through these comforting patterns we have set for ourselves. These first-time triggers can sneak up on us and completely disrupt our lives. We can think we are doing OK, and then suddenly we're triggered back into the grief and loss.

These first-time experiences do not have a time limit. It is easy to understand this happening for the first year after a loss. The natural cycles of the seasons, traditions, and holidays throughout the year will be affected. Sometimes, it is several years later when you engage in some activity for the first time since your loss. There isn't something wrong with you if you get triggered when this happens. It is not a regression in your grieving process. It is just a random first-time experience that reminds you of who, or what, you lost.

I have also found that if you were still in the shock or fog when you experience a first-time event after your loss, it may not seem as impactful as when you experience it outside of the shock. The first time you are mentally and emotionally present, and out of the fog, is when these events seem to hit the hardest. Like I had mentioned, you may be doing well and then get triggered suddenly without warning. So be prepared if the second time you experience something really feels like the first, and the worst.

It doesn't always have to be an established tradition or event that is affected. It can be a dream you had for yourself, and now you must go through life without the whole picture of what you had hoped for. There are multiple ways we can get triggered, by first experiences. We don't really have a choice. We will get triggered, and we will be reminded of our loss. After we experience the trigger is when we have a choice. We have the choice to deny our emotions, distract ourselves, self-protect, or even begin to identify ourselves with the loss we experienced. We also have the choice to confront our grief and process our emotions. Some choices are better than others.

I believe it is important to confront the emotions in these triggering experiences. It is not something to be afraid of; it is just something to be aware of. If we are willing to confront the pain and grief in these events, and allow ourselves to grieve, they won't have the same level of trauma and pain the next time. Little by little, we can transition from focusing on the loss and begin to experience life again. As we continue to experience these events, traditions, or holidays each year, the pain and grief will decrease. It is not about forgetting—it is about living. You can live, thrive, and be happy again. You don't have to forget to be free.

I am not saying that after the first experience everything will be great the next time, but I have noticed that the firsts are the worst. Each consecutive time we re-experience an event, there are new aspects of that event that are changing and growing. We begin to adjust to the new normal, and our focus on the pain of the loss is not as intense. We can slowly reconnect to the good memories attached to the event, and who or what we lost.

The events of your life will never be the same after your loss. It will be different. As we grow and change, so do our experiences. If you are repeatedly experiencing the trauma of the loss with the same intensity as each trigger or event happens, please get some professional help. It is possible to live again, to thrive again, and to experience joy.

If you need help with these triggers, you may want to sign up for my free email course that trains you with tools to live a lifestyle of freedom*. You will learn how to implement the Three Steps to Life when you trigger so you can intentionally stay present, confront your thoughts and emotions, connect with God, and resolve your triggers. It is a simple course that many have found helpful.

* www.faithbygrace.org/three-secrets

CHAPTER SIXTEEN

SOMETIMES WE NEED A BREAK

We have been looking at the need to intentionally face our grief head-on and process our emotions. Now we are going to look at the benefits of taking a break from grief. Allowing yourself to rest and take some time to breathe will greatly help you in your grieving process.

It can be difficult and exhausting to intentionally face your grief and process your pain after a traumatic loss. Just surviving the grief is a lot to handle. As we find ourselves in the midst of it, it is easy to forget about personal health. It can take all you have to just get through the day. The idea of self-care might be a completely foreign concept.

Allowing yourself to take a break and care for your mental, emotional, physical, and spiritual needs is an essential part of establishing a new normal. Self-care is an important aspect of the grieving process. Grieving is work, hard work. Continually working hard without a break can cause additional problems and bring on even more hardship. Even God demonstrates a time of rest in Genesis 2, when He rested from all the work He had done. Then in Exodus, He introduces the idea of Sabbath rest.

> Remember the Sabbath day, to keep it holy. Six days you shall labor, and do all your work, but the seventh day is a Sabbath to the LORD your God. On it you shall not do any work, you, or your son, or your daughter, your male servant, or your female servant, or your livestock, or the sojourner who is within your gates. For in six days the LORD made heaven and earth, the sea, and all that is in them, and rested on the seventh day. Therefore the LORD blessed the Sabbath day and made it holy.
> – Exodus 20:8-11

Rest is a blessed and holy time. The Lord wants us to rest. In Mark 2:27, the Word tells us, "The Sabbath was made for man." He created that time for us to be able to rest, recover, and live in peace. A time of rest will help us be able to think clearly and have more peace of mind.

A traumatic loss can take over our entire thought life. We can get lost in contemplation and enter into a very painful and stressful internal world. Taking a break helps your mind temporarily disengage from all those thoughts, in a healthy way. This will help you to get reacquainted with the world around you.

Taking a break is not the same as denial. Taking a break and allowing yourself time to relax, have some fun, or experience something adventurous is not denial. This time will help you to see that you do not have to do this alone. You are not alone in this. The Lord is acquainted with your grief, and He is able to help you. Here is a reminder from Chapter Four:

The Lord is acquainted with, knows, has experiential knowledge of, and comprehends our grief. He has received, accepted, lifted, and carried away our grief and sorrow. He knows your grief, understands your situation, and can help you with your sorrow.

These times of rest in between the times of intentionally facing our grief, and processing our pain, will help us let God be the one who carries our sorrows. It will help us reset our perspective and begin to see God's hand in the process more clearly. Our world will get bigger than our loss, and we will slowly be able to see it. We will begin to see beauty again in places we did not think possible.

You may find it difficult to rest at first. It can even feel like you are being neglectful because you are not focusing on and feeling bad about your loss. Just like every other aspect of grieving, I recommend giving yourself the time you need. Rest as much or as little as you can. Each time you allow yourself to rest and take a break, you will find it easier to do. These times of rest are a small experience of practicing how to live in your new normal. Little by little you will be able to experience life and be freer.

Take your time and do what you can. Re-engaging with society after a loss can be overwhelming. I am not recommending that you push yourself past what you feel safe doing. There were many times when I could not even go in public after experiencing loss. After our home burned, I had a weird sense of social anxiety in my body that I could not even explain. Even though my loss had nothing to do with crowds or public spaces, there were times when it was difficult to go in crowded public spaces. I would sometimes not engage with things that I did not feel safe engaging with. Little by little, I would engage as I could. It is OK to rest at home if it is too much for you to be in public. There is no need to pressure yourself. I recommend doing something you feel safe doing, something that will help you disengage from your grieving for a time, so that you can rest and rejuvenate.

While grieving a loss, we may be tempted to comfort ourselves in unhealthy ways. Self-care is not the same as self-medicating. When I mention self-medication, I am referring to the unhealthy ways we try to numb, deny, or distract ourselves from the emotional pain and grief. Taking care of our mental, emotional, physical, and spiritual needs is not an unhealthy distraction. If we take the time to care for ourselves, we will be able to face the grief.

It can be tough to get motivated to do "regular life" while grieving. You may not have any interest in it. Trying to do something fun, in the middle of all the pain, might not even be a concept that you can grasp. However, I think it is very helpful to remind yourself that there still is fun in the world. Even small moments of experiencing fun, joy, or excitement can help us and strengthen us. Try to take advantage of those moments when you feel inspired. The joy of the Lord is our strength.

Be strong and courageous, you can do this. Take some time, let yourself breathe, enjoy the moment, and commend yourself for the work you have done. You are so much stronger than you know.

CHAPTER SEVENTEEN

HOPE RESTORED

The grieving process isn't just about grief. It is about establishing a new normal where you can live and thrive again. As we confront our emotions and the pain from the loss, the fog begins to lift, and we slowly begin to have clarity of mind restored.

As we move through the grieving process, one of the many experiences we have will be a restoration of hope. These flashes of hope can seem unusual and even out of place sometimes. Depending on the level of impact from the loss you experienced, there can be a sense of sadness and hopelessness that can set in while grieving. The depth of sadness that can happen after a loss sometimes makes it seem completely hopeless that you can ever feel anything other than grief. Having a sensation of hope return in the midst of this pain can be a very weird experience.

When a moment of hope is restored, it is almost like the sun breaking through the clouds on a gray, overcast day. It brings light to an otherwise dark and sad place. In the beginning these moments can be random and fleeting. One moment you can be grieving, then you blink your eyes and find yourself feeling hope; you blink again, and you're back to grieving.

As we looked at in Chapter Three, grieving is a very unstable process. You may not even be in a place where you are experiencing any type of hope. That is OK. There is not something wrong with you if you cannot even comprehend the idea of hope right now. Just know it can happen, and it will happen, as you confront your grief and process your emotions.

There is no set time for when you may experience hope again. Everyone goes through the grieving process in their own way, with different intensity, different timelines, and different emotional responses. Take your time; there is no hurry. Let yourself grieve, let yourself feel your emotions, and allow yourself the time you need.

As I write this, it has been almost a year since we lost our home in the fire. It has been an interesting emotional ride. While grieving this loss, I've experienced hope in several different ways. The first time, as I'd mentioned, happened early on when my children found the burnt remains of the title page of Chapter Eight, "Repent and Believe", from *Identity Restoration*. This was a flash of hope in the midst of tragedy. Even though it didn't fix anything, it was a beautiful moment of hope where I felt loved. It was a glimpse of God's goodness, and a reminder of normalcy outside of the trauma.

While I was still in the fog after the loss, hope would come and go. There were times when I would wake up in the morning and it was like nothing bad had happened. Of course, soon after that, all the thoughts and emotions from the loss would flood in and remind me that something bad did happen. This was almost like re-experiencing the loss over again. Even though the feeling I woke up with didn't always last, it began to give me hope that things could be different.

The hope we have is not a hope that life will return to what it was and be the same again. We already know that life will never be the same. The hope we experience is a hope of life, joy, peace, freedom, and love. Hope is a natural state of our true identity. The hope we experience is an aspect of our character in Christ that has been refined as a result of the endurance produced in our suffering.

> Therefore, since we have been justified by faith, we have peace with God through our Lord Jesus Christ. Through Him we have also obtained access by faith into this grace in which we stand, and we rejoice in hope of the glory of God. Not only that, but we rejoice in our sufferings, knowing that suffering produces endurance, and endurance produces character, and character produces hope, and hope does not put us to shame, because God's love has been poured into our hearts through the Holy Spirit who has been given to us. – Romans 5:1-5

As we experience the grace of God in our suffering, the endurance will reveal the character of hope that is our true nature in God. This hope is in God, the love of God, the goodness of God, and the nature of God. This hope will not put us to shame or disappoint. Sometimes after a loss, we can get distracted and get our hope misaligned or misguided. We may be tempted to put our hope in certain outcomes or circumstances that are not the Lord. Unfortunately, this misdirected hope is not an aspect of our character in Christ and it will be disappointing and sometimes shame-producing. The Lord will not shame you in your grief. He is there to comfort you and restore your hope.

It is not about getting over it. It is more like getting through it. We need to take it day by day, and sometimes just moment by moment. The days will become weeks, weeks will become months, and months will become years. As you allow God to meet you in the middle of your grief, in whatever timeline works for you, you will begin to be able to move through it and establish your new normal. It is not the time that heals, though we may need time to heal.

You have what it takes to get through this. The love you have is what will allow you to endure, to hope, and to believe again. Your ability to endure and hope is the expression of your love. If you didn't love, you wouldn't be able to endure your loss.

Love bears all things, believes all things, hopes all things, endures all things. – 1 Corinthians 13:7

Celebrate the hope you do experience. Hold on and endure in the love of God when there is no hope. God's love has been poured out into your heart through the Holy Spirit. His love, and your love, are the reasons you can hope again.

You will hope again. You will thrive again. May God's grace empower you through love!

CHAPTER EIGHTEEN

ABILITY TO BE HAPPY AGAIN

Happiness is not the first thing most people think about when thinking about grieving. With the pain, loneliness, and sadness that can result from a traumatic loss, happiness isn't even a consideration sometimes. It is understandable that you may not even be in a place where you can consider happiness yet. That's OK.

While grieving, there is no process of trying to be happy again. We cannot force it or rush it. We can't make it happen on our own. Happiness is a sense of pleasure and contentment that comes from the Lord. It will begin to return. It is possible to be happy again.

Righteousness, peace, and joy is within us. The Word tells us in Romans 14:17 that the kingdom of God is righteousness, peace, and joy in the Holy Spirit. In Luke 17:21, the Lord tells us the kingdom is within us. We do not need to seek for righteousness, peace, and joy outside of ourselves or in our circumstances. God has imparted these realities into us through Christ, by the power of the Holy Spirit. These are normal for us.

The Greek word used for **joy** in Romans 14:17 is Strong's G5479 – **chara**. It means gladness, cheerfulness, and calm delight. This foundational gladness, cheerfulness, and calm delight is already in us. Our losses cannot take that away. This is the contentment and pleasure that is always available to us in Christ.

Even though our losses and circumstances cannot steal the true joy and happiness that is an aspect of our identity in Christ, they can cause us to disconnect from that reality. The trauma of experiencing loss can shake us at the depths of our soul. Remember, we were not created to experience loss. It is not part of the kingdom. We will never have who or what we lost back. The loss we experienced will always be a part of our lives, it just doesn't have to be what defines our lives.

In the beginning of the grieving process, we had to remind ourselves that maybe we could be OK again. As we process our emotions and thoughts and begin to accept our new normal, we slowly return to a sense of being OK, and believing we will be OK. It doesn't mean we won't have bad days and we will no longer get triggered into the grief of our loss again. We just won't get triggered as often or as intensely.

The intensity of grief we experience can cause a lot of confusion about our lives and our identity. When we lose something or someone we had a deep, intimate connection with, it can affect what we believe about ourselves. Trying to understand our identity apart from who or what we lost can be a very painful and confusing process. As we recover from a traumatic loss, we slowly begin to think clearly and reconnect to who we truly are.

Unfortunately, sometimes the pain we experience can cause us to identify ourselves in the loss itself. Others may even begin to identify us in connection to our loss. I still remember how things changed after our home burned. Instead of just being introduced by my friends as, "This is my friend Ray," it became, "This is my friend Ray. He just lost his house in a fire." At first, I did not notice it. I was in the trauma bubble and the loss was such a huge part of my life. Shortly after the loss, it started to become weird. I still do not fully understand the reasoning behind this habit. "Hello, here is my friend, and this is the latest traumatic loss he has experienced." It was a weird experience to be identified with my loss that way, and it made trying to engage in normal life even more awkward.

As tragic as loss can be, it does not establish or change our identity. One of the key aspects of being able to be happy again after a loss is getting to know ourselves for who we truly are, separate from our loss. We are who we are, with or without who or what we lost. A deep, meaningful aspect of our lives is gone, but we are not! If you are having trouble understanding who you are without who or what you lost, there is help available. A grief counselor can help you process your loss. You could also get to know yourself better and allow your heart to have choices through an Identity Coaching Session with someone on our team.

Yes, it is possible to be happy again. As we process our grief, we will reconnect with the truth of who we are and begin to experience life again. The joy and peace that are a natural state of our identity in Christ are unshakable. We can never lose these. As we reconnect with our true selves, we will begin to reconnect with things that brought us happiness before our loss. This is sometimes a slow and uncomfortable process, but it can and does happen. There is no proper timeline for this. We all need to process how we process, and reconnect to our joy and peace as we can. Allow yourself the grace and time you need.

It is possible that, as we begin to experience happiness and contentment again, a feeling of guilt can happen. A common lie that my coaching clients experience is that it is somehow disrespectful, dishonoring, or uncaring to be happy after a loss. Being happy is not disrespectful or uncaring to someone you lost. It doesn't mean that you haven't been deeply impacted by their absence. This can be tough as you start experiencing joy and happiness again. It can feel strange to sense your heart moving forward without them, and you may find yourself resisting this at first. Returning to your true nature in Christ after a loss is not dishonoring to the memory of who or what you lost.

As we move through the shock and fog of loss and begin to think clearly again, we can reconnect to all the aspects and qualities we loved about who or what we lost. It will allow us to enjoy our memories and celebrate all the good and wonderful things we once had before our loss. This does not happen smoothly, easily, or quickly. This is a messy process where we can go from happiness to sadness, to joy, to guilt, to loneliness, and back to happiness again and again. This is an example of the emotional roller-coaster ride we looked at in Chapter Three.

Continually facing our pain, emotions, and thoughts in our grief can be hard work. Thankfully in Colossians 1:11, the Word tells us we have been strengthened with all power, according to His glorious might, for all endurance and patience with joy. Having the ability to persevere through grief does not come from our own strength and willpower. Our ability to endure through the grief and experience joy again is through the strength and power that God has given us. You can do this; you can experience happiness and joy again. You can have fun again. You can live and enjoy your life again. And if that's not where you are today, it's OK.

If you feel safe and emotionally ready, try this exercise. Take a moment and let yourself relax, breathe, and connect to the presence of the Lord. When you feel His comfort and presence, ask the Lord to highlight an aspect or memory of who or what you lost that will bless you and bring joy. Let yourself experience the good feelings that helped you to love and appreciate who or what you lost. Take your time and enjoy all the good things as much as you can. Remember to stay aware of the presence of God and let Him comfort and guide you. It is OK if this also stirs up emotions of grief. Celebrate what you can, and process what you need to.

> May the God of hope fill you with all joy and peace in believing, so that by the power of the Holy Spirit you may abound in hope. – Romans 15:13

CHAPTER NINETEEN

THE PIT OF SELF-PITY

One of the greatest hindrances to processing our grief and establishing a new normal of freedom, peace, and joy is self-pity. This mental focus will sabotage our natural healing process and keep us stuck in an exaggerated experience of the grief.

All of us will experience a sense of self-pity at some point during our grieving process. Self-pity is what inspired Chapter Twelve, Grieving the Loss of a Good God. I believe this is a more common experience than we may want to admit.

Just like the depression, hopelessness, sadness, or any of the emotional experiences that can get triggered while grieving, self-pity is something that may come and go during the process. This only becomes a problem when we get triggered into self-pity and we stay there. This will keep us engaged in all the painful emotions and hinder us from reconnecting to and experiencing the good aspects of who or what we lost.

There may be more than two, but over the years of coaching I have seen two common ways that we get off track from our natural grieving process and get stuck in self-pity. The first one happens when we get hyper-focused on how the loss affects us personally. It is natural for this type of thinking to come and go during the grieving process. As I said, the problem is when we get singularly focused on this and get stuck on that path. This will transition the grieving process from being a time of healing into an establishment of victimhood. Once the victim status is established in our mind, we will begin to hold on to the pain and build upon it. It will keep us from being able to process the pain in a healthy way. Instead of being able to be present in our grief, think our thoughts, feel our feelings, and allow God to meet us in those, we will begin to protect that painful area of our hearts and not let healing in.

The second way I have seen my clients get off track from their natural grieving process is by establishing their identity in the loss itself. This is commonly aided by the culture around us. People are usually uncomfortable around someone who has experienced a traumatic loss, and they will treat that person differently. I mentioned this habit in the last chapter. As people around us start identifying us with our loss, it can encourage us to begin to do the same. People's awkwardness, along with the confusion that comes from loss, can distort our understanding of our true identity. We can begin to think and refer to ourselves in a way that identifies us in the loss, or in the effects of the trauma. I believe there needs to be an intentionality of thinking that does not allow our loss to become our identity. Without this intentionality, we can unconsciously settle into a false identity.

If the loss becomes your identity, then unresolved pain, grief, and hurt will be a natural expression of that identity. Instead of processing the pain and moving toward freedom, peace, and joy, the pain, grief, and hurt will become accepted as your new normal. Your loss is not your identity. Yes, you experienced a traumatic loss, and it will affect the rest of your life. You went *through* the loss; you did not *become* the loss. You are an overcomer filled with freedom, peace, and joy in the Holy Spirit. If you make the loss your identity, it won't be possible to be free from it. You will continually be stuck in a loop of the grief, pain, and hurt until you no longer identify with it.

Not identifying with the loss does not mean you have to forget or separate yourself from who or what you lost. You never need to forget, and you probably never will. If you identify yourself in who you truly are, as a child of God, you can experience the strength of the Lord and persevere through the trials of loss. If you cannot understand how to not identify yourself in the loss, while not separating from who or what you lost, I recommend you get help through coaching or counseling.

Let me remind you that you don't need to be healed of the grieving process. Grieving is the healing process. I believe grieving is a natural process that will occur in us unless there is an unnatural disruption to the process. The unnatural disruptions are lies that we believe either before, during, or after the loss. For example, if you believed being a victim was your identity, that would be a lie. Regardless of what trauma happened in your life, your identity will not change. You always were, and always will be, an overcomer and a child of God.

I have personally coached many people in successfully processing their grief and moving forward. When helping someone with a trauma or a loss that they seem to be stuck in, I help with two specific things. First, I help them identify any lies they were believing from before the loss that are keeping them from being able to process the loss. Then, I help them identify any lies that were established in, or because of, the loss that may be keeping them stuck in a loop of self-pity.

Once they are able to identify and repent from any lies, they are naturally able to process the grief. Now, let me be clear. This does not magically make all the grief go away. This allows them to now begin the grieving process instead of just being stuck in the pain and hurt. Although this is very freeing, it is not always a fun time for the person. It can be very emotional for someone who must begin the grieving process after they realize they have been stuck in a loop of self-pity and unresolved pain. This can be especially difficult if they have been stuck in this loop for a long time, while thinking they were grieving.

The sooner you allow yourself to grieve your loss, the better. Remember, you can do this. As a child of God, you have what it takes to persevere through your loss.

CHAPTER TWENTY

LIFE OUTSIDE THE TRAUMA BUBBLE

At some point during our grieving process, our lives begin to grow bigger than the loss we experienced. This is a transitional time when our lives are becoming more stable, our minds are becoming clearer, and our emotions are becoming more balanced. This is life outside of the trauma bubble.

When we experience a traumatic loss, it seems like we are trapped in an overarching bubble of trauma. It's a cloud that follows us everywhere we go. This cloud is the culmination of all the different aspects of grief that we have already examined. The fog, the sensitivity, the hopelessness, the loneliness, the sadness, and the emotional roller-coaster ride all create this overall sense of trauma that affects us mentally, emotionally, and physically.

In the beginning of the grieving process, it feels like grief is all-encompassing. The dark cloud of trauma seems to cover and touch every aspect of our lives. At some point as we are processing our grief, there is a moment when everything seems to shift. The fog lifts, the hopelessness decreases, and the sensitivity to loss becomes less intense. This is the start of life outside the trauma bubble. This aspect of the grieving process is when we can look around and see our lives more clearly. We will begin to reconnect with our lives and start moving forward.

The concept of "life outside the trauma bubble" came to me through conversations with friends after the fire. When we would see someone we had not seen since the fire, it was like they were experiencing our loss as if it had just happened. Their compassion and love for us was encouraging, and they were truly devastated for us. The problem with this was, we were not experiencing our loss like it had just happened. We had been processing the loss for a while and were not in the intensity of grief we once were. I did not want to be drawn back into the intensity of the grief they were experiencing for us. To help them understand where we were in our process, I started letting people know that we were "outside of the trauma bubble."

Living life outside of the trauma bubble does not mean we are done grieving. This just means we are now in the stage of grief when we can accept the loss, start experiencing other aspects of our lives, and find our new normal. We will still be affected by our loss and experience the different nuances of the grieving process. It is just a time when the traumatic feel of the loss is not as overwhelming.

The ability to live outside of the trauma bubble is directly related to how much we have allowed ourselves to be present in our grief, process our thoughts and emotions, and reconnect with our true selves. As we looked at in Chapter Eighteen, your loss has not changed your identity. The loss you experienced did not cause you to lose the freedom, peace, and joy that is a natural aspect of your identity in Christ. Any of the fear, shame, or guilt that is keeping you from moving forward in your grieving process is a result of lies.

The truth is, you can be free, experience peace, and have joy again. You will be reminded of your loss, and you will still experience the pain and sadness of the grief. This transitional time of accepting the reality of your life, and reconnecting with who you truly are, is very important in finding your new normal. This acceptance and connection will establish the quality of your mindset, allow you to be in touch with your feelings, and help you to be present in your life.

This is a time when it feels like you can breathe again. A time when you are not constantly bombarded with the weight of your grief. You can even start connecting again with the hopes and dreams of your life. A new determination begins to set in, and you can begin to feel more stable. It can even feel odd to feel OK. A significant part of this stage of grief is an acceptance that it is OK to be OK. There is not something wrong with you because you are able to be happy again. You have permission to live! Giving yourself permission to live, and to thrive, will transform your life.

At this stage of the grieving process, we are transitioning from being connected mostly through the pain and grief, back to being connected by the aspects of why we loved and cared for who or what we lost. We are more able to talk about and celebrate the things we loved. It is also a time when we can move from a false sense of idolizing who or what we lost and be able to see more clearly all the aspects of our relationship, including the things we didn't really appreciate. Being honest about the real relationship you had, or the actual experience you had, is not disrespectful. Remember, denial is not going to help you heal.

There is no need to create a false sense of perfection of who or what you lost. Trying to focus on only the positive, or only the negative, will not help us. I have seen both of these strategies used by my coaching clients, and ultimately it doesn't help them face reality and grieve accordingly.

You may even feel some sense of relief now that you are outside of the trauma bubble. This can be a very touchy subject. I still remember years ago, when I was first starting out in ministry, someone I was mentoring committed suicide. I had only briefly started working with this person, but I got to see the depth of the misery and pain that they lived in daily. It was miserable. After the suicide, I was talking with my pastor and I mentioned that along with the grief of this loss, I had a sensation of relief because they were no longer suffering. I was corrected immediately. I was told that I should never feel relief in a situation like that, and having that emotion was inappropriate. After being shut down so strongly, I started looking at my response. I even went to a counselor to work it out. I found out that feeling relief was a completely normal and common response to a loss. We will have all kinds of emotional responses to loss, and they don't always make sense. Adding guilt and shame to your grief will not help you heal. I am thankful that I went to a counselor and was able to process my feelings.

Since then, over the years of ministry, I have worked with many people who experienced relief, along with all the other emotions, in their grieving. I have continually experienced people guilting themselves and feeling ashamed because of any sense of relief. The false religious spirit is doing everything it can to steal, kill, and destroy your identity, authority, and community. The shame and guilt from the false religion we encounter can cause us to be afraid to share what we are truly feeling. This can potentially derail our grieving process and keep us stuck in a loop of fear and condemnation.

There is no set standard of how we should experience grief, or what emotions we should or should not feel. God can handle any emotion we have. Even if we have thoughts that may be sinful, He already knows them, took them to the cross, paid for them, and is not condemning us for them. I do not believe it is God's will, or in any way helpful, to condemn ourselves for not meeting some false religious standard that has been established. We just need to give ourselves permission to feel our feelings, think our thoughts, and let the Lord meet us in them.

If we let cultural or religious "shoulds" control and limit our responses and emotions after a loss, we will establish lies and begin to protect ourselves with fear, shame, or guilt. One of the ways I have helped my coaching clients in their grief is to help them identify the lies they believe that are connected to the loss. Some lies were established before the loss, and they keep people from being able to process their grief. Some are established because of the loss, and they keep people stuck in the unresolved pain. Some of the "shoulds" are the lies. Identifying the lies, giving your heart a choice, repenting, forgiving, and believing the truth will help you naturally be able to grieve. You will be able to process your loss and experience freedom, peace, and joy.

You can love again.

You can dream again.

You can hope again.

You can live again.

You can do this.

CHAPTER TWENTY-ONE

YOUR NEW NORMAL

Your new normal. It is not what you hoped for. It is not what you wanted it to be. It is what you have. You have made it through the shock, the fog, the emotional roller-coaster ride, and all the different trials of a traumatic loss. Now you get to move forward and live your life.

Getting to this point in your journey is a major accomplishment. It has been difficult work to intentionally stay present in your thoughts and emotions, process your loss, and let yourself grieve. Your willingness to be vulnerable with yourself, God, and those you trust has allowed you to get this far. Congratulations, this is a very courageous achievement!

This has been a long and painful journey of what seemed like many victories and many failures. There is no celebration at the end of this journey. It may not even feel like you have accomplished anything, but I promise that you have. As time passes, people are less aware of your loss, and may not even be as available to help you. Unfortunately, even though others go back to their lives, your journey does not end. You will be in a continual transition of loss, grief, adjustment, acceptance, restoration, and life. You may never "get over" your loss, but you are getting through it, and I am proud of you!

The loss you experienced can be an inspiration for growth and strength, or limitation and weakness. The loss itself will now be a part of your story. This is another key point of choice in your life. We have looked at the many different choices and options through your grieving journey. You have made some healthy choices, and most likely some unhealthy. Each choice has brought you to where you are now in your grieving process.

Whether it feels like it or not, you are wiser, stronger, more equipped, and more in touch with yourself because you persevered through your grief. Even though I do not believe that your loss was God's will or His plan for you, I do believe He will use it for your benefit. I have seen God's redemption repeatedly in my client's lives. The wisdom you have acquired through this process has equipped you to handle other trials and trauma in your life.

Being equipped to process grief is not the same as being prepared for loss. Processing through our loss does not prepare us for future trauma. We are never really prepared for loss. No matter how many times we go through the grieving process, it will be challenging and painful. Processing grief and loss is some of the most difficult emotional work we will ever have to do. The courageous work of intentionally facing our emotions and our thoughts in the midst of our pain and loss, will equip us with the tools we need to be able to help ourselves and others who are grieving.

It is OK if you feel like you haven't accomplished anything. You might still feel beat up, tired, sad, and alone. It is OK if you do; you are not the only one. The emotional roller-coaster ride continues. It just isn't as extreme and scary as it was in the beginning. As you bounced around through the grieving process, it was more like you were processing one thing at a time. Piece by piece, you worked through your loss. Now you can see it more holistically.

Once we are out of the trauma bubble and moving forward with our lives, we see the holistic nature of our loss, and this comes with its own challenges. One of these challenges is when we look back over our grieving process and start questioning and judging how we handled it. This is similar to what we looked at in Chapter Six. The difference is, now we are reviewing what could have been different after the loss, rather than what could have been different before. Unfortunately, this is a common response I have seen with my clients. Reflecting on our grieving process and judging ourselves will not help us move forward.

You did the best you could in the situation you were in. This is not the time to be hard on yourself about choices you made, or how you handled your grief. You are where you are, and there is no need to question and judge yourself. Just getting through the shock and trauma of a loss is a significant accomplishment. So much of the grieving process affects our ability to think clearly and make decisive choices. As much as you can, let yourself be reassured that you did the best you could, and that is enough. You can be proud of your work.

You have done well and have survived your experience so far. This has been a tough journey, and though it seems to have somewhat settled, the journey continues. As you move forward and live your life in this new normal, you will look back with fondness, excitement, love, anger, sadness, and heartbreak. The painful emotions and thoughts that are triggered will still need to be confronted and processed. As we discussed earlier, the intensity of the wheel of emotions will be less, but you may still get triggered. You will miss who or what you lost, and you will still grieve your loss.

Just as you were able to accept your loss, now you get to accept your life. The same perseverance that allowed you to work through the grieving process can now help you thrive in your new normal. There will be new challenges and opportunities for growth and healing. You can do this. You have what it takes to be able to thrive.

In one of the lowest moments of my life, I asked God, "Why do I have to keep living?" He simply replied to me, "Because you are not dead." Most of the conversations I have with the Lord consist of very straight-forward, direct answers like this. I get some of the deepest revelations from some of the simplest answers from the Lord. This encounter led me to two different Scriptures.

> I shall not die, but I shall live, and recount the deeds of the Lord. – Psalm 118:17

> I call heaven and earth to witness against you today, that I have set before you life and death, blessing and curse. Therefore choose life. – Deuteronomy 30:19

These two Scriptures were an inspiration for me to choose life, to live, and to thrive. It was not always an easy choice to choose blessing and recount the deeds of the Lord. Sometimes I just wanted to wallow in my self-pity and look at all the things that have gone wrong in my life. In my upbringing, I was trained to look at what was wrong and complain about it. It has taken a lot of perseverance and intentionality to retrain my thinking. For so much of my life, I allowed the bad things to define me and misalign my focus. This wrong focus affected how I saw everything and created a narrative of sadness, depression, and loneliness. Being intentional about choosing life has helped me to become more familiar with joy, gladness, and loving connection with others.

This new outlook has empowered me to be present in the current moment, feel my emotions, and be aware of my thoughts. Allowing yourself to stay present in the moment and experience what is actually happening is a powerful tool to help you live and thrive in your new normal. Continually looking back and regretting your past losses, or looking forward and being afraid of future losses, will not help you. Regret and fear will keep you from thriving. If you find yourself getting stuck in these loops of regret and fear, remember there is help available. You don't have to fight this battle alone. Going to a grief group, seeing a counselor, or having an Identity Coaching session can help.

Regardless of what the enemy has stolen from you, he cannot steal the freedom, peace, and joy that is the natural aspect of your identity in Christ. Remember, you are who you are, and the enemy can never steal that from you. You are loved, powerful, courageous, and free. Your loss does not define you—your God does. You are equipped with everything you need to live your life, pursue your dreams, and be free.

> And God is able to make all grace abound to you, so that having all sufficiency in all things at all times, you may abound in every good work. – 2 Corinthians 9:8

You have all the grace and sufficiency you need to abound and thrive in your new normal. May God bless you as you continue your journey and live your life.

Freedom is available.

Peace is possible.

Joy is real.

Thank you for trusting me
and allowing me to be
a part of your journey.

Blessings and peace as you
continue to process and
heal from your loss.

Kay

RECOMMENDATIONS

For help finding your identity separate from who or what you lost, and for help with your grieving process:
www.faithbygrace.org/identity-coaching

For help finding a grief counselor:
www.psychologytoday.com

For help finding a grief group:
www.hospicefoundation.org

RESOURCES

MY RESOURCES

Identity Restoration
If you desire a lifestyle of freedom, peace, and joy—this is the book for you! It is a culmination of over 15 years of in-depth study and real-world experience, that has been refined into a lifestyle of freedom that you can easily implement. You will be equipped with practical and sustainable tools to help you go from a false normal of fear, shame, or guilt into a kingdom lifestyle of freedom, peace, and joy, in any situation or circumstance. Be equipped and empowered to know who you are, believe who you are, and live out the fullness of that truth in the power of the Holy Spirit. Freedom is available!
www.faithbygrace.org/identity-restoration

*Who Do You Think You Are? Bible Study –
Volume One*
Each session of this Bible study will help you
discover the truth of your identity in Christ
according to the Scriptures, and equip you
in identifying and unraveling what you truly
believe about yourself and God. Statements of
faith are given to help you partner with the truth of who God
says you are. You can know the truth, believe the truth, and live
the truth. This transformational study will help you do that!
www.faithbygrace.org/who-do-you-think-you-are_bible-study

*Who Do You Think You Are? Devotional –
Volume One*
Each day of this devotional will help you
discover:
• The truth of who God says you are according to
His Scriptures • Any mindsets or beliefs that are
keeping you from living the truth • Statements
of faith to remind you of your redeemed, alive, pure, fruitful,
righteous, and accepted identity in Christ • How your life can be
transformed by believing the truth of who you are • Practical steps
you can take to believe and live in your true identity in Christ.
www.faithbygrace.org/who-do-you-think-you-are_devotional

OTHER RESOURCES

Good Grief – Granger E. Westberg
Good Grief is a simple, easy to read booklet that I have recommended to hundreds of people over the years. It offers great insight on the emotional and physical responses people may experience during their grieving process. This is an excellent resource to have in your library.

The Practice of the Presence of God – Brother Lawrence
There are multiple versions and reprints of this book. The copy I read years ago looked like this. Practicing the Presence of God was the book that originally introduced me to the idea of focusing on the presence of God. I so enjoyed the simplicity of Brother Lawrence's understanding and explanation of allowing yourself to be aware of the presence of God in your everyday activities.

Made in USA - North Chelmsford, MA
1045306_9780996698931
01.20.2020 1447